Psychotherapy
and the
Uncommitted Patient

Psychotherapy and the Uncommitted Patient

Jerome A. Travers, Editor

The Psychotherapy Patient Series
E. Mark Stern, Editor
Jerome A. Travers, Associate Editor

The Haworth Press
New York

Psychotherapy and the Uncommitted Patient has also been published as *The Psychotherapy Patient*, Volume 1, No. 2, Winter 1984.

The Haworth Press, Inc., 28 East 22 Street, New York, NY 10010

Library of Congress Cataloging in Publication Data
Main entry under title:

Psychotherapy and the uncommitted patient.

    "Has also been published as The psychotherapy patient, volume 1, no. 2, winter 1984"—T.p. verso.
    Includes bibliographies.
    1. Commitment (Psychology) 2. Psychotherapy patients. I. Travers, Jerome A. II. Stern, E. Mark, 1929- . III. Title: Uncommitted patient. [DNLM: 1. Psychotherapy. W1 PS87 v.1 no.2 / WM 420 P97536]
RC569.5.C65P79 1984   616.89'14   84–19754
ISBN 0–86656–371–7

Psychotherapy and the Uncommitted Patient

The Psychotherapy Patient
Volume 1, Number 2

CONTENTS

Psychotherapy
and the
Uncommitted Patient

Awakening Responses in the Uncommitted: A Preface and a Challenge

Welcome to this second issue of *The Psychotherapy Patient.* Dr. Jerome Travers has brought together a significant collection of articles which as a group make a meaningful attempt at illuminating the dynamics of uncommitment.

From personal observation it has become clear to me that the uncommitted patient can, with proper help, eventually learn to develop accommodating, reasonable, and altruistic resources. Unlike the emptiness of noncommitment, the uncommitted state is never totally indifferent to the potential of a concerned life. Looking closer still, the uncommitted stance is often the culmination of an aborted search for personal meaning. Noncommitment, on the other hand, belies any reciprocal connection to the larger social community. Uncommitment, as a personality attribute, suggests a nagging hopelessness in the presence of emotional challenges. Feeling no hope, the uncommitted person may recognize neglected opportunities for commitment, but recoils from them because of having no realistic ways of expression. If noncommitment amounts to a total lack of concern, then, by contrast, uncommitment indicates oppressive fear and lack of direction.

Uncommitment, as an attribute of the psychotherapy patient, is to be regarded as a calling card, not an ultimate diagnosis. The therapeutic dyad was established to create a significant confrontation with the possibility of greater commitments. As a process, the psychotherapy relationship provides a workable methodology to understand and eventually to help surmount the obstructions which stand in the way of meaningful commitments.

It has been the sincere hope of the editors of this journal that this multidimensional analysis of the uncommitted patient will help the practicing psychotherapist to better appreciate the challenges which are presented with ever increasing frequency in his or her work.

E. Mark Stern
Editor

Introduction:
Keeping Promises and Other Quaint Values

What began as simple musing turned into an investigation of a most complex phenomenon. What is one to make of persons who only come for one session or a few sessions, or have a different therapist every few years, or have continual therapy but with different therapists, or who appear to be both patients and nonpatients? Is it always resistance, lability, or premature termination to leave a therapist after a few weeks, months, or years? Are we locked in to models which presume therapy to be more interminable than terminable? Is being committed really a prerequisite for therapy?

Any discussion of the attribute of uncommitment often leaves one speechless. In his review of the literature in his article in this issue, Dr. Willis shows that any investigation of uncommitment turns up dust. Even the classic study of alienated youth of the '60s, *The Uncommitted* (Kenniston, 1964), refers more to the American Ishmael reacting to and rejecting the American culture. Kenniston's study was an examination of the detached observer of the overexamined life, a fragmented self who is strong in opposition but weak in affirmation. Yet even in this stimulating book, the intrapsychic issues of uncommitment remain untouched.

When a colleague said, "How do you expect me to write about uncommitment when I'm already leading that life-style?", I sensed that something more than a raw nerve was touched. The pattern of emotional wandering, of moving in and out with therapists and others, began to form into a wider question: Why do people so often find it hard to commit themselves to a task or a person? Within this context lie the related issues of keeping one's word, holding confidences, fulfilling obligations, making sacrifices, and going the extra mile.

Have these old values, plus the ability to say "yes" or "no," and being wholehearted, melted in the warmth of the humanistic movement? Are the patterns of the uncommitted patient's life to be seen as pathology or are these patterns part of a heightened microcosm of a society undergoing identity diffusion (Erikson)?

The authors in this issue have drawn on their specific expertise and interests, as each examined this important patient phenomenon from his or her perspective. It is from this multiplicity of perspectives that light gets shed on this attribute. It is our hope that you are left, not speechless but stimulated.

Jerome A. Travers, Ph.D.
Associate Editor and Editor of this Issue

REFERENCE

Kenniston, K. (1964). *The uncommitted: Alienated youth in American society.* New York: Harcourt Brace & World.

Clarifying the Issue:
The Issue of Clarity

Jerome A. Travers

Rows of corn partially hid the half dozen large white buildings on the horizon. It was outside Canterbury, New Hampshire, last summer, that we had come, my family and I, to visit with Shaker Eldress Gertrude Soule, one of the last Shaker sisters living there. She greeted us warmly, her face smooth, her eyes twinkling, and her gait jaunty. At age 93, she was one of the youngest remaining Shakers. A remnant of a group led from England by Mother Anne Lee, these last Shaking Quakers (1781-present) were originally part of a sect, the United Society of Believers; at their height, 1830-1840, they had 6,000 members in 18 villages throughout the North East.

I wondered what it must be like to be the last; to know that your community will be no more; to see your lineage end. What kept her so cheerful, radiant of health, generous in manner? Her aliveness and intactness reminded me of the many nuns that I had known growing up: not the neurotics presently portrayed on Broadway, but more the Ingrid Bergman's of *The Bells of St. Mary's*; those women who had dedicated their lives to running orphanages, schools, old folks' homes, as teachers, nurses, and administrators. I thought of my two high-school friends who have been working unselfishly for a quarter of a century, easing human misery: one in the Amazon region, the other in India. The common adjective describing them was "dedicated," models to emulate. Certainly many had conflicts and turbulent lives, but who hasn't?

Sister Gertrude, at age 21, signed a Shaker covenant, pledging to become part of a larger community, her new family. Nuns, too, took their vows, committing themselves to a life of service and sharing. In this manner, each found worthwhileness and meaning in her life. Why did she make such an impact on me? Partially because her form of commitment is so rare. The last two decades have seen a special concern for growth, openness, process, experimentation, moving on, letting the river flow by itself, doing one's own thing, finding oneself, "and so it goes." What had

Jerome A. Travers, Ph.D., Guest Editor, is a consulting editor for *VOICES: The Art and Science of Psychotherapy* and the *Journal of Pastoral Counseling*. He serves on the Executive Council of the American Academy of Psychotherapists and is in private practice in Summit, NJ.

started with eternal promise seems to have elided into lability, confusion, and ambivalence. With some irony, this year's commemorative stamp marking Martin Luther's 500th birthday is a silent reminder of possibly the last time someone publicly took a stand.

What did Sister Gertrude have that David, my most intractable patient, doesn't? A feminized, Howdy Doody-looking 37-year-old, David longs to be Dorian Gray: remaining eternally youthful while watching his visage age, his quest for eternal youth. He dropped out of high school to be a rock 'n' roll star, developed the persona of various movie stars, yet continues to work at menial jobs while maintaining a vivid fantasy life. Almost two decades later, his constant questions are: "What should I do with my life?", "Who am I?", and "Should I be gay or straight?" His intense loneliness is abated by fantasies and furtive activities: peep shows, porn movies, go-go girls, and flirtations with homosexuality. Any real relationships with women fizzle, partly due to his intense self-involvement, an observing ego which only observes itself. Additionally, his passivity and ambivalence with women and his emotional stiltedness with them usually drives them away in both confusion and frustration. His relationships don't end; they just seem to drift away.

David's father remains emotionally absent in his life; and to his mother, who wiped his behind until he was seven, David remains bound. His weekends are solitary: often drinking, visiting different churches, teasing himself about the sexual proclivities of whomever he meets. He comes to therapy and opens each session with, "I have nothing new to say" and "Why am I here?" He remains committed to therapy but not to change. David falls into that obsessive-compulsive style which, Andras Angyal (1965) says, "make up the bulk of those patients who fail to be substantially helped by therapy, sometimes with a succession of therapists over many years" (p. 197).

David's life follows profoundly what Angyal calls the "pattern of noncommitment," a holistic way of viewing the neurotic complaint of obsessive-compulsions. Angyal's thesis, which I hope to spell out, is that the pattern of noncommitment is the outcome of an abiding confusion as to whether the world is basically friendly or inimical (p. 157). This painful state of uncertainty leads people to respond to significant others with both hostility and love. Their struggle is against confusion as they search for slogans to live by.

This dilemma of noncommitment is originally caused by the inconsistent behavior of a significant adult, in which the child finds it impossible to find a way to gain acceptance. Because rewards and punishments were based on parents' moods, the child never knew if he or she would be indulged or mistreated. David was indulged by his mother, who was downputting at the same time. He interpreted her hovering attentiveness as a sign of her not caring, that is, she had no confidence in his ability to handle tasks appropriately. Instead, he was overwhelmed by arbitrary double messages of approval and disapproval.

From the trauma of inconsistency, says Angyal, the child's loving impulses become more deeply hidden than hostile impulses (p. 136). It is safer for a friendly orientation toward the world to be deeply hidden. The bind is completed in that the child's love and hate are directed at the same object. Consequently, any significant situation may arouse these two sharply conflicting attitudes. Imagine how David feels when his mother sends him a regular supply of skin cream so that he will attend to his acne. When asked, he responds with a confused smile.

David's ambivalence, which permeates everything, originates in the radical split between his confident and distrustful orientation. His confusion, with its double-minded orientation, is expressed in pathological doubt and indecision, in an inability to be wholeheartedly involved in anything. Because love and hate pervade all areas of his life, none of his actions are backed up by his whole personality.

David's two conflicting orientations are reflected in his inhibition of action and emotion; crying is his major emotional release. Indecision has become his life-style, and his range of possibilities in any decision is usually reduced to two polar opposites. In this state of habitual tension, ultimately no emotions, except anger and fear, are consciously experienced, let alone expressed. His skin problems reflect the turbulence of his soul.

On entering my consultation room, David gives a sheepish, baleful, sideways look—an inhibition of his aggression and a signal of his hostile orientation. Even his curiosity has a hostile quality, and popping up between his remarks are grudges, vengeance, fault-finding, and a tone of spitefulness. David fails to see how his actions and attitudes have consequence and social and interpersonal effect. Even though he describes himself grandly in movie-star terms, his self-contempt is so fundamental that he doesn't believe his grandiose self-image. In this struggle of polarity of feeling worthless versus feeling valuable, he turns any evidence of self-worth into its opposite, thereby developing an intractable negativism.

David's loving and hopeful orientation is permeated with guilt feelings. His tender feelings toward family and friends threaten him in this life-and-death struggle of hostile and loving feelings. For him, loving and wanting to be loved are signs of weakness and an enormous threat. Angyal reminds us that, paradoxically, such pervasive sense of guilt is the only unmistakable manifestation of his loving orientation toward people (p. 184). His guilt is not neurotic but is instead an appropriate affect related to his ungenerous behavior.

We might note that David's state of constant confusion is more painful than anxiety; his life is an attempt to gain clarity and thereby reduce the tension of doubt. His attempts to dispel confusion lead to a kind of doubling, a dividing everything into polarities, an either-or thinking, which simplifies and violates reality. As David cannot proceed in achieving a lasting separation of his twin orientation, the black *or* white for him then becomes black *and* white, the root of his paralysis. And as he searched for something stable, some rules to live by, all his spontaneity became squelched. He entered therapy in search of a guarantee of foolproof rules for behavior and with belief in the miraculous, painless powers of the therapist.

David remains stuck, the antecedent to depression, to the extent that he refuses to venture out into the unknown, for to do this is to risk losing his few satisfactions. His pattern of evading risk and growth is through non-commitment, a saying "yes" and "no" at the same time; often, this is shortened into "yes, but." Because he cannot identify himself with his action, he does not commit himself fully to any course of action. His stabs at personal freedom are masked ways of avoiding commitment. In his relationships, his compulsive search for a partner is the "yes" of the dilemma; the "no" is the equally compulsive flight, lest he get "trapped" in a relationship. Such a pattern of noncommitment, based on his abiding confusion, results in an inability to give himself to any career, cause, or relationship.

David's life pattern, then, reveals the symptoms of the pattern of noncommitment: his essential lack of feelings; his outspoken need for independence and personal freedom; an uneasy sense of inner detachment; and his refusal to share with his partner or anyone.

My work with David encountered difficulties, which Angyal says, arise from three sources:

1. David's extreme self-derogation and his despair about himself;
2. the coactivation of opposite tendencies, polarities, resulting in extensive intellectual and emotional blocking; and
3. pervasive guilt feelings, which work against the improvement of self image. (p. 197)

David's basic self-contempt and extreme self-derogation keep him locked in guilt feelings. One thrust of our work lies in the uncovering of his latent healthy patterns, in a discovery of his healthy parts. The key to our work is to provide for him a firm personal basis for self-esteem. This work goes on in a holistic mode: uncovering and establishing his psychological pattern, during which time the neurotic pattern is dominant. As his neurotic pattern and healthy pattern begin to equalize in strength—the crucial stage for a struggle for decision—there is a wavering of two ways of life which claim his allegiance. During the terminal period of successful therapy, a healthy pattern is in ascendancy as David masters the difficult task of staying well.

David's therapy has a death/rebirth motif: a demolition, followed by despair, followed by reconciliation. The task of demolition involved showing him the hopelessness and futility of his way of life. This is intended to lead to a bankruptcy of his neurosis, which he experiences as his own bankruptcy. The core of the experience of bankruptcy is despair, and associated with it are other forbidden emotions: specific fears, intense general anxiety, and an acute sense of guilt (p. 227). It is this experience of despair which is *the* crucial step leading out of such emotional dysfunction. This despair is the feeling and conviction that he cannot move anywhere anymore; that he just cannot continue living the patterns in which he has been living. David is aware of his attitudes common to all neurosis: pervasive fear, hostility and anticipation of hostility, self-derogation, the lack of genuine fulfillment, and the distortion of inner and outer reality. His task now is to see his own unique persistent pattern of behavior, his pattern of noncommitment as his global statement.

At the same time, as the task of demolition of the dysfunctional pattern is going on, so also is the task of reconciliation occurring. This required finding a fulcrum outside his neurosis, the healthy roots of his neurotic trends, in order to loosen his neurotic organization. This means eliciting his healthy pattern within his neurosis. This fulcrum involved, for David, his love of art, his love of travel, his genuine kindness and good will, and his capacity for absurdity.

We shared the turbulent journey, wherein David could transfer onto me the image of his primal parents, during which he could see me alternately as the mythical enemy and also the answer to his wish for an all-giving magical helper (p. 321). After sharing his guilt and shame feelings and discovering that he was not being blamed, David gradually noticed that my attitude was based neither on blindness nor on moral indifference. Feeling valued and respected, David slowly discovered that he was being seen, with all his shortcomings, as a likable and worthwhile human being.

Getting well is only a prologue to staying well. Each requires courage, that first of human qualities because it is the quality which guarantees all the others. Angyal reminds us that all analysis is merely preparatory, for "when the patient is ready to face the issue of his basic orientation, he has had enough analysis" (p. 273). After this, the central neurotic issue, the choice between trust and distrust, between stagnation and movement, gets decided on a global scale.

What can David still learn from Sister Gertrude about staying well? His proud autonomy, his concern for freedom and independence, will only leave him incomplete and self-involved. To be, says Angyal, is to mean something to someone else. We only come to life by being understood and acknowledged by someone else. The worst punishment, he says, citing William James, is to be unnoticed by everyone (p. 18).

In focusing on his needs, David has forgotten that he wants *to be need-ed.* He has yet to discover that self-respect is heightened by being of value to another. What Sister Gertrude and the nuns of my youth have, and David doesn't have, is community and an in-tunement with transcendence, a sense that life is more than oneself. They spent their lives living in an affectionate relationship and participating in the life of others with all its joys, hopes, and disappointments, and becoming part of a unit by extending themselves beyond themselves. Participating in another's life implies not just romance and pleasure but also sharing and suffering. David, through shifting from a life-style of uncommitment to one of health will discover that "loving means that one's life is larger but not necessarily easier or more pleasant" (p. 24). It is toward a largesse of spirit and expansiveness of possibilities that he is moving.

David continued to strive for mastery (autonomy), while often forgetting that he needs and longs for participation (homonomy). Such homonomy is the wish to be in harmony with a unit that one regards as extending beyond one's individual self. No wonder that my high-school missionary friends are full of boundless optimism and good humor, and have a genuine joy in their work with the disadvantaged. David's therapy work, the goal of which is the full emergence of the pattern of health over the pattern of neurosis, and a balancing of the trends of autonomy and homonomy, is not yet complete.

Sister Gertrude's life serves as a silent witness and model for David in the integration of these two trends of autonomy and homonomy. Her life has been spent in the celibate, religious, utopian tradition of the Shakers. She has lived in their ascetic life-style, without vanity, emphasizing brotherhood, communal work, and communal sharing, and finding satisfaction through her work. Men and women living together by choice in a celibate life-style, the Shakers experienced that the spiritual, individual, and communal were continually affirmed in their labor.

While David wonders what to do, Sister Gertrude is off to put up preserves for her neighbors. She smiles at us and waves good-bye.

'Tis the gift to be simple, 'tis the gift to be free,
'Tis the gift to come down where we ought to be,
And when we find ourself in the place just right
'Twill be in the valley of love and delight.
When true simplicity is gained
To bow and to bend we shan't be ashamed
To turn, turn, will be our delight
'Til by turning, turning, we come 'round right.

Simple Gifts
Alfred Ministry, 1848

REFERENCES

Angyal, A. (1965). *Neurosis and treatment: A holistic theory.* New York: John Wiley & Sons.
Kanter, R. M. (1972). *Commitment and community.* Cambridge, MA: Harvard University Press.

An Unexpected Greeting

Michael Eigen

For many years I was a committed patient of the most fervent sort. I entered therapy with all I had in me, with a painful sense that I had little to lose. It was true I had doubts as to whether I *really* could be helped and, if so, in this way. Eventually therapy became an important part of my being. My major therapy ended (unresolved) when my therapist left the city in the wake of a divorce and collapsing life of his own. And I became a committed therapist.

I soon encountered uncommitted patients and was taken aback by the possibility that not everyone was as interested in giving as much of themselves to therapy as I. It was difficult to grasp that some people preferred to hold on to their lives before therapy, even when the former seemed to offer very little advantage. I began to ask myself what made this possible and passed my patients before my mind's eye in a more questioning way.

First, there was a young man who called himself a Dufus. He was married with two children, yet felt himself getting nowhere in life. He seemed to be sincere and warm and he put a lot of effort into not liking himself. He had been in therapy twice before and claimed he had received little help. He was his same old uncommitted self, in a job he didn't like, essentially drifting. He was afraid he didn't have it in him to do something on his own.

I felt bad that he felt so bad about himself and wished I could help him see himself in a better light. But I soon came up against a basic stubbornness, something rock-like and immovable, which made me feel I was banging my head against a wall. I began to think he wanted me to be in his corner, to encourage and pick on him, but also to feel how exasperating a life can be. His past therapists must have felt something similar. They doubtless played a role in the minimal viability of his marriage and his ability to sustain himself as a family man. They gave him permission to be an affectionate husband and father. Yet he left them without seeming to give them a chance to show what therapy could do, just at the point of barely getting started. Did they know how they helped him?

Michael Eigen, Ph.D., practices in New York City. He has coedited *Evil: Self and Culture* (to be published by Human Sciences Press) and is presently working on a book on psychosis.

He looked a little like Mortimer Snerd, just as he said. But he was kindly, not snide. Everyone in his family had always called him a Dufus. He felt they were right. He felt his mind was slow, yet tenacious. Once an idea formed he bullheadedly stuck to it, often with disastrous consequences. He was not at all nimble and could not reverse himself in midstream. He saw himself, too, as a horse with blinders on, in general, a beast of burden. I was tempted to convince him he was wrong, but realized he would best me. In fact he reminded me more of the retarded rather than schizophrenic children I had worked with. He probably had at least average intelligence.

I no longer recall how long he stayed with me, but it was under a year, part of the time in group therapy. He seemed to get something out of calling himself a Dufus in front of other people, a number of whom were quite quick. Most of the group members liked him. Everyone wanted to help. At some point he started to talk about buying a van and wandering around with his family and starting a business somewhere. And even if he failed to start a business, at least he would be on his own. He didn't make much money anyway, so how much worse off could he be? At least drifting might make an honest man of him. It would reflect the way he felt inside. And therapy? How could therapy help? This was his third try and he was still the same.

He announced he was leaving therapy as soon as he got a van and I never saw him again, but I spoke to him twice by phone, and some years later heard about him from another of my former uncommitted patients. She was a divorced young woman trying to make it on her own with two rough little boys. She was on the fat side and felt flattened by life. Her husband turned out to be a ne'er-do-well and, finally, violent. The men she met were weak, mean, and stupid. They lived off her welfare checks and, in the end, vanished. Her boys would get attached to them and then have to go through being alone with her again. She was usually depressed and on dope.

She spoke a lot about her sister who had every advantage—a husband who made money and loved her, two wonderful children, and leisure. Her parents favored her sister, yet she had more of a relationship with them, even if a very hate-filled one. Although she envied her sister, she also felt disdain. Her sister's life had always been too easy and lacked character. She had leisure for lovers and shopping, but what about her*self*?

Beth, my patient, was often late for sessions or didn't come at all. She had no money for sessions (she was on Medicaid) but went to lots of rock concerts. She met Dufus in group therapy and when he was saying (again) how once in his life he would like to feel and do something smart, she found herself thinking (saying), ''I want to kick one of these bastards out before he leaves or, better, get along without him moving in in the first place.'' Therapy ended soon after the great Woodstock rock concert. She said her going there was one of the most important things in her life, one of the few things she ever really did for herself. She was proud of the way she was there, although I never exactly learned why. Apparently she felt herself more important, more of a person. Was it simply the confirmation she got from seeing so many like-minded people all together? Hadn't this occurred at other concerts? Why this place? Why now? The mystique of Woodstock, something special, a *magna carta?* It was a voice that came in waves throughout the '60s.

I ran into her last year in an art shop in my new neighborhood. She said hello, but at first I didn't recognize her. She was sitting behind the counter and looked splendid, a really nice, enlightened woman. When she got up to talk with and help me, I saw she was fatter than ever. She told me Dufus wasn't so dufus anymore. He owned a restaurant and had a family of six, with his oldest child married. He would soon be a grandparent. As I was leaving, she asked me if I saw clients in the neighborhood, but I had to say my office was a borough away. I offered to give her names of therapists who worked nearby. She said she knew of people she could see, if she wanted to. She showed a feeling for me I never knew she had (transference or not)—a glimpse of how much our time together had meant, what a life-saver it turned out to be. And yet I sensed her pride in having done it her way. We see each other on the street or in the store she works in from time to time and have exchanged a wide range of unfaked glances and greetings.

It may be banal but still very real to say that such incidents (and there are many, of all hues) drive home the importance of the therapist being able to derive his or her sense of importance from nothing very tangible. The unknown and perhaps unknowable is a constant therapeutic medium. It is a pleasure when out of this silence (or worse) a friendly word makes an unexpected appearance. But the sound of one hand clapping goes on out of earshot, and the retort of trees in the forest is heard by someone.

Hazards of Being a Sixteenth Psychotherapist

Naomi James

A little less than 2½ years ago an attractive, bright 43-year-old woman sat in my office for the first time. As her story unfolded she announced, "You're my 16th psychotherapist." A deluge of feelings and images momentarily caught me off guard. When I recovered my equilibrium I asked her if she was aware of the impact of her statement. I suggested that she was trying to tell me something very important about herself. She seemed puzzled, then in a rather matter-of-fact manner added, "I'm hoping to find a therapist who can really understand me. At this point I am totally disillusioned with the entire process of therapy." Needless to say, I felt little reassurance from her response. My first impulse was to back away from such a formidable challenge. If I accepted this woman in therapy I would have to acknowledge that I was only one of a potentially endless procession. Yet the possibility that I might be the "best" of the series pulled the strings of omnipotence somewhere within me. Being one of the series is not new to me—I am the youngest of six children. As I grew up I sometimes fantasized that I was the best of the lot in one way or another. To be the last therapist in the life of this troubled woman, however, was to accept the reality that the therapeutic journey we would share was sure to be strewn with remnants of all of her therapies. Could I survive the alluvium of feelings, resistance, and transference?

I have chosen to write about Ellie, as I shall call her, for two reasons; first, her life reflects so well the theme of this issue of the journal. Second, I think I have the opportunity to state a good case for the use of Object-Relations Theory to support assumptions about her intrapsychic and interpersonal functioning, especially the issues of noncommitment and obsessiveness in a borderline personality. Although it is difficult to write about someone still in therapy, the clarification that follows from putting my thoughts in better order has had beneficial effects on both of us. I struggle to balance my personal reactions with sound theoretical grounding as we work together. Turning to respected colleagues for consultation has kept me in touch with the dangers that may lie in my need to have

Naomi James, Ph.D., is a clinical psychologist in private practice in Venice, CA.

17

Ellie "complete" a therapy with me. To be the last of a series for the wrong reasons is ultimately destructive to my client and to me.

Ellie's history as a psychotherapy patient reaches back over 30 years. She first saw a counselor when she was in her early teens. Some of the therapies were interrupted because she moved but others were terminated for reasons which are still unclear. Ellie attributes the failure of most of the therapies to the faults and lapses of the therapists. She blames them for the continuation of her problems. They were insensitive, or punitive, or perhaps they were regarded as less intelligent than she. Ellie's descriptions of her experiences in therapy, as well as her accounts of current life events, have been laden with projection. As we proceed in therapy now, distortions of historical material are gradually undergoing reevaluation and I am arriving at a clearer picture of how Ellie has moved in and out of therapeutic relationships.

Whatever distortions may have occurred, it is clear that the fabric of this woman's life has been woven of pain and disappointment. From early childhood she felt constricted and controlled. She sees her mother as having been emotionally unavailable and aloof. Her mother's subtle and unverbalized criticism seemed to have permeated every corner of Ellie's existence. There was no touching, no physical comforting, no love exchanged between the two. Ellie felt a constant pressure to quietly conform to make her mother's life easier. Caregiving activities usually associated with good mothering were absent from Ellie's life so she attempted to care for herself. She recalled with reawakened humiliation her daily walk to school in mismatched, unironed, and unmended clothes. She felt ugly and believed other children laughed at her behind her back. To compensate for feelings of worthlessness she became hostile and aggressive toward schoolmates. Ellie was, indeed, an ostracized and lonely child.

I first became aware of the extent of splitting used as defense against abandonment depression, when Ellie described her relationship with her father. Just as she experienced her mother as all bad and uncaring, so too, did she hold a picture of her father as the possessor of all things good. It is apparently true that whatever loving attention existed for Ellie did come from her father. He took her on outings, read to her at bedtime, and awakened in her an intellectual curiosity and cultural sensibilities. With him Ellie felt special. However, from time to time memories emerge which reveal split-off intense negative affect toward him. These negative memories bare the critical, perfectionistic, and sometimes violent side of her father. When pressures to mold herself to parental expectations became too much for her to bear, she threw tantrums. Father then responded with swift and harsh retribution. Ellie has had to split off from awareness all of her own feelings of rage and helplessness in order to preserve, untarnished, the only experience of tenderness she can summon up from her painful early years. We have only begun to touch upon the mourning process which will help Ellie face the loss of something which really never was.

Ellie's need to avert criticism moved her to finely tune an ability to avoid decisions and to leave, unfinished, projects which were begun with great energy and eagerness. What to others seemed like involvement in too many ventures, was her method of staying uninvolved. The pattern of initial enthusiasm followed by loss of interest suffused every area of her life except school because in academic success she had assurance of a positive response. Ellie has developed an acute sensitivity to the expectations and reactions of others. I have observed her scrutinizing my every facial expression, every body movement for the slightest betrayal of disappointment, disagreement, or criticism. When she cannot confirm these feelings in me, she accommodates her projection to my demeanor. "You're hiding your real feelings." If we are successful in breaking through the projected stream of unacceptable internal imagos, Ellie experiences both sadness and relief. For a brief period she tolerates the intimacy that stems from our cooperation; she softens and smiles. Later, clouds of suspicion again fall across her face.

When Ellie was 18 she left home and shortly thereafter married. The couple moved from their home town in the East to the Midwest, settled down, and started a family. Before she realized that her marriage was foundering, Ellie had borne three children.

Old patterns of interaction returned like ghosts. Ellie, who had longed for a mother's love, sought mothering from even her youngest child. She was drained by her children's ordinary needs. Ellie had learned to camouflage her own emotional hunger by projecting it onto others. She saw her husband and children as insatiable and therefore dangerous to her well-being. Recognition of the repetition of dynamics of her nuclear family brought remorse, but the predominant feelings of anger and resentment always returned to cover it. Bitter arguments punctuated each day's family interactions. Ellie began making threats to leave the family but at the brink of decision, gripped by anxiety, she would change her mind.

When her children were in their teens Ellie finally left, announcing her intentions to enter graduate school and to live on her own. She applied to a graduate program, was accepted, then decided it was not the right program for her. A second program followed, then a third. After less than a year, pressured by financial need, she returned to work. Although Ellie remains at this job she obsesses about whether her decision is the right one. She has begun several creative professional endeavors only to lose interest at the first sign of difficulty, or on the brink of success.

Lingering uncertainty and indecision mark all of Ellie's life choices. Friendships last for brief months. On initiation of a new relationship she is intensely involved and preoccupied with the other. At the first hint of disapproval or nonsupport Ellie seeks greener pastures. People, she has concluded, are either out to extract something from her or they hold no value because they have little to give.

Theoretically, there are several issues in this case which interest me, but one best captures the essence of the bind that produces a stance of noncommitment. I use the word "stance" deliberately because obsessiveness and noncommitment are purposeful positions. Ellie used them much as a boxer employs weaving and bobbing. She developed these defenses to disguise her individuation needs during the critical rapprochement subphase of separation-individuation (Mahler, Pine, & Bergman, 1975). As a toddler, having been denied the right to a mind of her own, she buried her individuation under a blanket of indecision and evasiveness, which later became hallmarks of her personality.

I find it helpful at this point to refer to the literature to cast light on obsessive and noncommittal behavior in general, and in the borderline personality in particular. Salzman (1968) has described the obsessive personality with great clarity, especially in regard to the dynamics involved in the therapy process. He has cautioned therapists that a traditional "do nothing until you consult with me" position is ego syntonic with the client's psychopathology, for it works paradoxically against the intent of therapy, that is, that the client becomes autonomous. He suggests that therapists work with the conflict in process rather than the actual alternatives embedded in the obsessional process. David Shapiro (1981) develops this idea by presenting clinical vignettes in which he illustrates how therapist and client become ensnared in the obsessive process. Unless the therapist is in touch with possible countertransference involving his or her own rigidity of character, the client's progress will be hopelessly bogged down in exploration of endless options.

Much of the literature on the obsessive personality focuses on neurotic process wherein the defense serves to keep unacceptable libidinal content repressed. The defense is seen as arising during the anal stage of development. But the anal stage spans the same years as rapprochement. Borderline pathology has been linked to a faulty transit of this stage (Masterson, 1981). Then how is the therapist to understand the function of obsessive behavior in each of these situations?

The neurotic's relatively well-integrated ego can tolerate insight without fragmentation so that the client is able to form a working alliance with the therapist. In a client with borderline pathology, pressure to make decisions, whether internally or externally applied, may lead to unbearable anxiety, depression, and suicidal ideation. This is so because ego structures are not fully consolidated and fragment under stress. Therefore, working with a borderline client requires particular sensitivity to the optimal level of the client's functioning. We must support healthy attachment and simultaneously promote individuation. On the one hand there is a danger that the client will become inordinately dependent upon the therapist. Individuation is halted as the client looks to the therapist rather than to self in choosing alternatives. On the other hand, if unsupported or if pushed prematurely toward autonomy and commitment, the client will abandon therapy.

The ability to choose a course of action and to follow it through is developed during rapprochement. It is during this period that the "good-enough mother" (Winnicott, 1981) will foster or inhibit exploration and will be available for refueling. If she cannot tolerate the loss of symbiotic attachment to her child she will discourage any movement toward independence. Her child will feel fear or guilt rather than excitement and enthusiasm and will opt for the safety of continued symbiosis as inner rage grows. The individuating child needs to feel free to move in and out of the mother-child universe. Ellie's problems with commitment are rooted in the dilemma she regularly experienced with her parents. Exploration and commitment to endeavors of her choice led to criticism and ridicule. Furthermore, Ellie could not approach mother for refueling because mother was not emotionally available. In Ellie's therapy history she has been unable to use her therapists for refueling for a variety of reasons, so she has returned to one after another hoping to find the emotional resting place which allows her to regroup her energies. She has become increasingly hopeless as she adds chapter after chapter to her therapy journal. Each new therapist is the recipient of accumulated hostility and suspiciousness.

I was very much aware of Ellie's need for a "good-enough mother" (Davis & Wallbridge, 1981) when she first began working with me. I was far less concerned with her hostility than with my own reactions to her need for perfect "in-tuneness." There are persistent questions at the front of my awareness. Would I be able to assist her in retracing and healing a faulty individuation process? Am I an instrument for her growth or am I a colluding partner?

A recent article in *Psychology Today* (1983, Nov.) addresses the ability of the borderline client to "hook" therapists and staff personnel in hospitals into a very destructive process. What I find missing in this article is reference to the therapist's contribution to the client's manipulations and rage reactions. When such a client focuses the need to connect with compelling intensity, the recipient of the communication may, indeed, be convinced that there is no one else who really understands the client better. Unless the therapist is alert to the seductiveness of such attention, an unconscious need to be the omnipotent complement to the client's incomplete self/object representation will be stimulated. Failure of the therapist to match the projection is inevitable. When this happens the client projects the "bad" internal object and relates to the projection from a split-off "bad" self.

We therapists are not blameless because we are part of the system that maintains such projective identification. Just as surely as our needs for validation lead us to provide a good fit for the client's projection of per-fection, so too, when we respond negatively from our own unresolved self/object issues, do we provide at least a small hook on which the client can hang the experience of "bad object." Projective identification cannot work unless both parties participate. If I feel confused or strangely "caught" it is probably because I have lost my ability to discern what is mine and what is my client's.

Jurg Willi (1982) has written an excellent book which, although in-tended to guide therapists in work with couples, advances the understand-ing of collusion in operation in any dyadic relationship. Willi outlines four collusive patterns, three of which are most pertinent to this discus-sion. They may exist simultaneously or serially or the couple may be stuck in one pattern of interaction. "Love as oneness in narcissistic col-lusion" involves issues of attachment for the preservation of self-esteem and wholeness. "Oral collusion" has a central issue of caring and nourishment and corresponds roughly to Mahler's practicing subphase of separation-individuation. Those of us who work predominantly with bor-derline clients most often see a pattern of anal collusion which involves issues of security, dependence, and autonomy. All of these concerns may surface from time to time in any couple. The interactions become col-lusive and pathological when partners become locked in polar, comple-mentary positions. One of the partners may cling to a regressive position, either forcing or allowing the other to take a progressive stance. My inter-est in Willi's model, aside from its use in relationship therapy, is its gen-eralizability to the therapy relationship. When therapy with a borderline client gets "stuck," a model such as Willi's provides guidelines to iden-tify my input into the unproductive process.

Willi refers to the passive-anal character as one "who accepts every-thing without commitment" (p. 100). That thought brings me back to my discussion of Ellie, but allows me to add another dimension to it. Work-ing with Ellie requires that I be sensitive to the manner in which she en-gages me because it reveals the type of collusion that she is seeking. If I take a regressive position consistently I stand the risk of repeating the pat-tern which existed during her childhood. I offer no direction or support and replay the mother who asked her to "hatch too soon," in Mahler's terms. Conversely, in the progressive position I rob her of her own voice. I demand that she conform to my expectations. Ellie would again find herself raging on the inside and performing on the outside.

How have I managed to keep an ongoing relationship with Ellie? I can-not say how I have differed from her other therapists. I am sure that most of them were as knowledgeable and as skilled as I. Perhaps she has re-mained in my care because of my respect for her process. Perhaps it is that I do not require that she stay in the process of the session, which replicates her mother's demand that she be her child's central concern.

We work with material which originates within the session and outside the session. I have been a consistent and reliable container for her rage, and I have been moved by her sadness.

Sometimes I wonder if what I am seeing and feeling makes much sense. It is then that I turn to my colleagues and to the literature to clarify my impressions. At times I must confront my countertransference; at other times I rest comfortably that others have traveled a road very similar to mine. My understanding of developmental theory has allowed me to assist Ellie in pushing the upper limits of performance without unbearable frustration. She is free to move at whatever pace she sets, and to retreat when regrouping of energies is necessary. Some therapists cannot tolerate this waxing and waning of energies and motivation in their clients. I believe their unwillingness to recognize lacunae in their clients' ego development leads to failure for both client and therapist.

Hellmuth Kaiser (1965) stated that it is the therapist who is entirely responsible for making therapy happen. The client need merely come to sessions. I have kept his words in mind, for they infer that we not only honor the client's existential state but that we know what countertransference reactions may impede our work. Kaiser has also said that the less integrated of the dyad will rise to the level of the healthier. This is a reminder to me that I am the therapist—that I pay attention to my own emotional health.

I cannot summarize my work with Ellie because it is still in progress. Only recently she suggested that I was holding her in therapy. She felt she was able to stop therapy. We had been working for over a month on her resistance to dealing with feelings about a recent visit with her father. I finally recognized that my pushing was strengthening her resistance, and I was wise enough to step back. After I had owned how I had been a part of this process, I told her that I believed that her therapy was far from finished but that I clearly acknowledged that it was she who must make the decision to stay or to leave. Ellie took a week off. Then she called me and said, "Who am I kidding, I need to come back." At her next appointment she was her old self; no major change had occurred. She thanked me for my ability to "put up with" her. Tears rolled softly down her cheeks.

Will Ellie ever be able to take a stand and stick to it? Will she ever be able to commit herself to a course of action? I hope so. At this moment I am happy to be holding my own.

REFERENCES

Davis, M., & Wallbridge, D. (1981). *Boundaries and space. An introduction to the work of D.W. Winnicott.* New York: Brunner/Mazel.

Kaiser, H. (1965). *Effective psychotherapy.* New York: The Free Press.

Kramer, R., & Weiner, I. (1983, Nov.). Psychiatry of the borderline. *Psychology Today,* pp. 70-73.

Mahler, M., Pine, F., & Bergman, A. (1975). *The psychological birth of the human infant.* New York: Basic Books.
Masterson, J. (1981). *The narcissistic and borderline disorders.* New York: Brunner/Mazel.
Salzman, L. (1968). *The obsessive personality.* New York: Science House.
Shapiro, D. (1981). *Autonomy and rigid character.* New York: Basic Books.
Willi, J. (1982). *Couples in collusion.* New York: Jason Aronson.

Comment

The position taken by Dr. James' patient Ellie in the therapeutic relationship exemplifies what Harry Guntrip (1969) has called the schizoid compromise solution. Dr. James refers at one point to Ellie's "method of staying uninvolved"; at another time to her "stance of noncommitment." She describes how Ellie leaves her husband and children, various school programs, a number of creative professional endeavors, as well as innumerable therapists. Friendships begin as intense involvements only to end after brief intervals. Guntrip has remarked that, "In proportion as a patient is schizoid, he is afraid of people just as much as he needs them" (p. 289). The essence of the schizoid compromise is to find a way of maintaining a relationship in a form that does not involve full emotional response. This can be achieved in a marriage, in a friendship, or in a job situation. A blocked analysis would be a very good example of this. The patient complains of being "stuck"; the patient may continue to come but does not open up any emotional issues for analysis; or he or she may leave and repeat the process with a new therapist. If the patient continues in treatment, there is the possibility of analyzing the forms of compromise which have been set up. But more than analysis of the compromise solutions is necessary to prevent the patient's leaving treatment prematurely. I will return to this point later.

If we take the thesis that every personality has to some degree a schizoid core of the self, then mental health, according to Guntrip and Winnicott (1975), would consist in having enough ego-relatedness and ego-strength to be capable of entering into and withdrawing from relationships with minimal fear: either of being overwhelmed by the other person in a close relationship, or of finding oneself profoundly alone, cut off, "empty" when privacy is chosen. In the latter instance the primary fear is of loss of the ego in a vacuum of experience. In the former it is the fear of losing one's individuality through submergence with those upon whom one depends (dependence in its healthy connotation) (Breggin,

1980). In the view of Winnicott and Guntrip, in normal maturational development a danger point may be reached as the infant begins to emerge from primary identification with the mother, if the mother does not provide adequate ego-support. The danger is not that the child's instincts will remain unsatisfied, "but that his basic ego-experience is lost" (p. 421). The experience of continuity in relationship with the mother "is primary. It is this relationship that brings into being an ego, a self that feels real" (Guntrip, 1969, p. 422). A weak, poorly formed self, a sense of "unrealness," an "emptiness" at the core, and accompanying terror that this small, weak, inadequately developed ego cannot stand up to life's everyday demands are concomitants of failure at this stage. Dr. James refers to her patient's "toleration" of the intimacy that "stems from their mutual cooperation." Following such an experience, the patient's "renewed suspicion" helps her to distance again from the closeness and reveals the degree of her "terror of intimacy." The patient's terror of intimacy betrays her basic ego-weakness, an infantile ego which she fears will betray her into the power of others through her dependent wishes.

Given the extreme importance of individuation issues—to use Dr. James' term—to the schizoid or borderline personality, then the very process of the "cure" necessary for recovery can be experienced as near to life-threatening, in that it "seems to require sinking his own personality in passive dependence on that of another person (the therapist), at least at first" (Guntrip, 1969, p. 308). It involves allowing oneself to depend upon and to be helped by the psychoanalyst. As the regressed, inadequately developed ego draws near to consciousness, the patient experiences extreme feelings of vulnerability and fright and a sense of "hopeless aloneness." If the patient can accept the protected, passive, dependent experience of the therapy, recuperation can take place and "rebirth of an active ego can be achieved" (p. 307).

Ellie's dilemma is that she cannot escape from her own need for compromise solutions, and she will continue in such a phase until her fears of relationship diminish and she can allow her needs to be met. As she finds Dr. James to be an understanding and reliable therapist and begins to effect a genuine therapeutic relationship, it will give her a chance to grow some deep-level security and to develop trust in her own capacity to protect her vulnerable self in relationships, particularly in the therapeutic one (Breggin, 1980).

The figurative "holding"* accomplished in the therapy with a schizoid patient is an essential part of the therapy task. Dr. James' frequent references to Ellie's need for "refueling" touched on this aspect, as well

---

*Of interest here is Winnicott's (1975) description of the mother "holding" her infant over a phase in living, that is, she "holds a situation so that the infant has the chance to work through the consequences of instinctual experiences" (p. 263). The situation is in some ways remarkably analogous to the holding work of the therapist with a schizoid patient.

as her reference to the "waxing and waning of energies and motivation" seen in her patient. Ellie's fear of submerging her ego, of loss of her personality, in relationship with the therapist must be constantly dealt with, as well as her fears that she will destroy the object (therapist). The schizoid patient feels a tremendous need to defend his or her freedom of self-determination and thus will remain (and rightfully so) on the defensive until the time when she or he has grown "enough" trust in the therapist. This will be a bumpy road to progress and the in-out program will continue to some degree almost to the end of a most successful treatment.

Kristina Lincoln, Ph.D.

REFERENCES

Breggin, P. R. (1980). *The psychology of freedom.* Buffalo, NY: Prometheus Books.
Guntrip, H. (1969). *Schizoid phenomena, object-relations and the self.* New York: International Universities Press.
Winnicott, D. W. (1975) *Through paediatrics to psycho-analysis.* New York: Basic Books.

Problems of Commitment
in the Psychotherapy Relationship

Lawrence Tirnauer

Problems of commitment are enormously complex and diverse. They affect every area of personal growth and personal stagnation, every stage of psychotherapy, and every facet of interpersonal relatedness. Furthermore, issues of commitment tend to be reciprocal and bilateral between the therapist and client, so that it is very difficult to understand a problem of commitment without understanding the therapeutic context in which it occurs.

The issue of commitment is really an issue of choice. It reflects a decision to either stay with some course of action, some way of relating, or to back away from that decision or thrust. Any decision to make a commitment (implicit or explicit) comes out of an assumption that more is to be gained than lost in making such a commitment. But one cannot ignore the fact that any commitment does involve some loss, some giving up of other possibilities and other choices. Often one needs to understand the threatened loss in order to fully appreciate the fear of commitment.

It is important to keep in mind that commitments may be experienced as either constructive or destructive. For one individual a commitment to finish a course of study, stay with a marriage, continue on in therapy, may represent a dedication to the individual's highest ideals and values. To another individual, those very same choices, those very same commitments, may feel quite destructive, and may represent the loss of values, the loss of cherished ideals, the compromise of a higher sense of integrity. To know whether a commitment is either constructive or destructive one needs to know the individuals, their struggles and the context of their life in which the commitment occurs. Breaking commitments may be destructive or a step towards growth.

We all have problems of commitment. We are all overcommitted to various negative aspects of our life, and undercommitted to various other positive aspects of our life. Problems of commitment do not represent a serious problem in themselves. They need attention when they interfere

Lawrence Tirnauer, Ph.D., is a psychotherapist in Washington, DC. He is a consulting editor of *Voices: The Art and Science of Psychotherapy.*

27

with forming worthwhile relationships, interfere with meaningful work, or interfere with the person's forming a more positive relationship to himself or herself.

Normal struggles around commitment represent an attempt to find some equilibrium when the needs and desires of the individual either impinge on the needs and desires of other individuals or conflict with other facets of one's self. Normal problems of commitment reflect a struggle in finding some balance between the needs for security (staying with the familiar) and the needs for growth, excitement, or adventure. Often there are no easy answers. For the therapist, a client's decision to stay in therapy may be taken as a constructive act, evidence of some maturity. Yet from the client's point of view the decision to terminate may reflect a willingness to take life more fully into his or her own hands, a decision to live life with more personal responsibility. And there may be validity to both viewpoints; each course may involve important gains and losses.

In the context of beginning psychotherapy, the patient's decision to keep an initial appointment may be seen by the therapist as a step in the direction of getting a better handle or perspective on one of life's many struggles, or a way of dealing with a crisis. Yet from the patient's point of view it may represent something enormously different. Thus keeping an initial appointment may reflect the acknowledgment that the patient is indeed crazy, sick, or emotionally disturbed. The decision to see a therapist may involve the breaking of a commitment the patient made to himself or herself "to be strong," or to "never see a therapist like crazy Aunt W did." At another level the commitment to keep an appointment may feel like the breaking of a commitment to the family to only discuss problems with other family members, or to never say anything critical about family members to someone who is not a member of the family. For the client, seeing a therapist may feel like the breaking of a commitment to the church or to higher spiritual values. The very decision to seek therapy often involves much more conflict, many more feelings of betrayal of old loyalties than we generally assume. It is generally much tougher for the client than even the client realizes.

Almost any issue in psychotherapy, any struggle around relatedness, can be conceptualized in terms of the issue of commitment. Issues of commitment do not just have to do with whether the individual *stays* in psychotherapy. Issues of commitment have to do with what course one holds oneself to in a relationship, and what is involved in the decision to hold to that course. Thus patients may stay in therapy for a period of many years, keep every appointment, always show up on time, pay bills promptly, and so forth, and yet act as if they had absolutely no commitment whatsoever to get to a better place in their lives, or a better place in their feelings about themselves. Underlying these surface commitments the client may fear that any movement in the direction of greater vulnerability is a step in the direction of becoming hopelessly insane, or a step in the direction of committing suicide. So the issue is only partially one of whether the patient stays in treatment. It is also a matter of what quality of relatedness the patient brings to the treatment situation, and the patient's fears and hopes about that relationship.

I have decided somewhat arbitrarily to discuss the theme of commitment in therapy around three broad issues in psychotherapy. There are many different ways to conceive of these problems. I have chosen those that I find useful to think in terms of when problems of commitment arise. The first issue I want to discuss is that of problems of structure and control. Here I hope to discuss not only problems of interpersonal control, but fears related to the problem of inner controls. Next I want to turn to issues of commitment that are related to the problem of having a "good" or worthwhile or valued Self, and the fears of intimacy. And finally I will turn to such issues as they relate to problems of loss.

Early in the treatment process commitment problems often arise around the issue of structure and control. The therapist typically sets a time, place, and payment schedule for the treatment relationship, as well as a policy about missed appointments. These are power issues. Can the patient accept the therapist's gaining this power around boundaries of time and money. To the degree the patient is anxious about not being in control of a relationship, to the degree to which the patient typically tries to control self and others through power struggles, issues of control will come up at this point. They will especially tend to come up when the therapist is anxious about taking charge of the relationship, is fearful of being in charge of the relationship with this particular client or with clients in general. It will also come up when the therapist tends to manage his or her own anxiety by becoming overcontrolling. Problems of control that get fought out interpersonally often are camouflaged attempts to maintain inner controls.

Developmentally, the child begins to gain control of inner processes at a point when the relationship to his or her mother (mothering one) is becoming more firmly established. Thus we see, for example, that toilet training is inextricably related to the child's confidence in the stability of the relationship to the mothering one. It is a common experience to have a loss of bowel control when there is a disruption in the relationship to the mother. An experienced child therapist knows that reestablishing a trustworthy relationship between child and mother is the *sine qua non* for dealing with the problem of loss of bowel control. Similarly in the adult, having confidence in the ability to regulate one's inner processes (feelings, imagination, body sensations, and so forth) is highly related to the degree to which one has established a caring and trustworthy relationship to another.

The paradox of therapy is that as the patient develops an increasingly positive relationship to the therapist, the patient's internal relationship to his or her *original* mothering one is deeply threatened, and there is a concomitant loosening of the ability to control inner processes. This then becomes a critical time in therapy. It is a time when patients may fear going crazy, and it is not uncommon for patients at such times to dream someone is being murdered or committing suicide (i.e., a giving up old internalized relationships). It is precisely at this point that the patient may wish to terminate: namely, when inner controls are loosening, and the patient is unclear whether he or she and the therapist have a sufficiently safe and durable relationship to tolerate the emerging feelings and memories that feel enormously threatening.

A client, after several months of work, decided he wanted to terminate treatment because he was "running out of funds." He had several large bills he wanted to pay, and he had not gotten a pay raise he expected. The therapist raised some question about terminating since therapy seemed to be going well, and early in treatment the patient had noted he had considerable savings, and finding money for worthwhile needs was rarely a problem. What therapist and patient needed to look at was how scary therapy was becoming because it was going well. The very act of establishing a positive relationship for the patient was not reassuring, but quite terrifying. Negative relationships were frustrating, but held a certain predictable security. A positive relationship, though, stirred many feelings, feelings of longing, feelings of fear, the reawakening of past hurts and past disappointments. The anxiety, guilt, and shame about these feelings became translated into an interpersonal battle, because the therapist was seen as a genuine threat to the patient's inner controls, and because it allowed the struggle to be fought away from the more frightening battle ground. To the degree that the therapist is anxious about setting boundaries around fees and time, it is easy to collude in the battle. To the degree that the therapist becomes anxious by the material beginning to surface, he or she may respond to the patient in ways that tend to confirm for the patient that the material is indeed too dangerous or threatening to surface in therapy, and the patient may react by terminating.

A different client threatened to terminate therapy when the therapy relationship deepened. She complained alternately that the therapist was probably wanting her to stay because it was profitable for him to do so, or alternately that she did not trust the therapist and considered him weak. In actuality what was happening was the therapist was becoming an increasingly important person in the patient's life. She now often found herself thinking about the therapist and therapy during the rest of the week. At times she had begun to feel the therapy was a threat to her marriage. More and more vulnerable feelings were surfacing, and she felt less and less in control of what was happening in the therapy hours. In her childhood family her mother had clearly seemed in charge of the family and to control things and make the important family decisions. Women were supposed to be in charge! By allowing the therapist to become increasingly important her identification with her mother, and the more familiar ways of relating to men was threatened. It was only by repeatedly focusing on her fears, her identifications, and the loyalties in a rather firm manner, that her felt need to terminate and thus regain control began to diminish. In so doing the therapist had to face his own awareness that part of him wished she would indeed terminate, because as the therapy relationship deepened he also felt much less in control of the process, was much more aware of all sorts of immature and primitive feelings arising in both himself and the patient. The major thrust had shifted from one around controls to that of fears of intimacy and of having a worthwhile Self.

We are all afraid of intimacy, because none of us is able to truly accept all of his or her feelings, thoughts, and fantasies in a loving way all of the time. We are all imperfect beings. We may project a notion of total acceptance onto some idealized image (like Buddha) or person. But notions of an all-accepting individual are not consistent with my notion of what it is to be a human being. So we are all afraid of intimacy to varying degrees, because we are all afraid or ashamed of some of our thoughts and feelings some of the time.

A number of years ago a colleague rubbed my foot in an affectionate manner. That night after I had fallen asleep, I awoke nauseous and on the edge of throwing up. Retrospectively, I was not ready to accept the homosexual feelings his action had stirred in me, feelings that I might now accept, be interested in, perhaps even wonder what might be beneath *those* feelings. Another time I found myself feeling very spiteful toward someone who was being very caring towards me, and I was feeling a bit ashamed of having those feelings. Today I might be more appreciative of the anxiety his affectionate feelings were stirring in me, and understand my spitefulness in more accepting terms. Not too many years ago I felt ashamed of feelings of contempt or moral superiority in myself, hoping that someday I might purge myself of what felt like very unacceptable feelings to me. Now I do not feel so intimidated by those feelings, and am more interested in how I and others deal with such feelings, not devaluing the very presence of such feelings. In the context of commitment, each of those feelings experienced might have stirred so much anxiety or shame in me that they could have seriously jeopardized the relationships in which they occurred.

Depending on the level of acceptance of Self, intimacy in therapy raises threats around the issue of commitment for client and therapist. While this may seem obvious, almost all of the therapeutic literature and popular literature supports the notion that people welcome intimate relationships, rather than fearing them.

Fears of intimacy are proportionate to the intimacy the individual has with himself, and the feelings of intimacy the person has experienced in prior relationships. To the extent the person has felt abandoned around his own feelings, increased feelings of intimacy in the therapy relationship become a threat to that relationship. I cannot emphasize too fully that this works for both patient and client.

One client with enormous struggles around any form of closeness to others dreamed that bombs were falling near him and the therapist, bombs that ''threatened to blow the two of us up.'' This dream occurred at a point where the client was very afraid of his own anger, and felt he needed to protect the therapist from it for fear of hurting the therapist. The therapist had come to represent in the transference his own Child Self, a Self which he could not then accept.

A different client reported finding it very hard to feel close to his wife. His associations led to the memory of feeling abandoned by his mother at a time he very much needed her, a time he had felt very close to her. Closeness now raised the threat of abandonment and betrayal for him. This client had abandoned therapy several years previously precisely at a point he had *felt* emotionally abandoned by the therapist. Now he was much better able to face those feelings and fears of abandonment and betrayal, rather than simply fleeing from them.

Another client said, ''I want to stay angry and depressed to keep people at some distance.'' This was from an individual finding it enormously difficult to make a commitment either in his marriage or in therapy. His dreams at this point suggested that closeness was associated with being homosexually penetrated. His self-esteem was too shaky at that point to look at either what might be behind the wish to be penetrated or the wish to penetrate others. At this same time in treatment the client talked about wanting to cut back in treatment or to ''cut it off'' completely, the therapy itself having come to represent a part of himself.

Clients frequently fear that emotional intimacy brings with it not a loving sharing, a source of nurturance or support, but rather the fear ''you'll discover all the garbage I have inside,'' or, ''my feelings will be too much of a burden for you.'' The latter fear is common with highly deprived people who fear the intensity of their neediness, consequently deny any feelings of dependency, and are therefore highly sensitized to even the slightest emotional withdrawal in the therapist. Sensing even the slightest emotional withdrawal, such clients then begin to withdraw themselves, becoming involved in a subtle dance of closeness, tantalization, fear, and withdrawal with the therapist.

As therapy progresses, and a client begins to develop both interest and friendliness to his inner experiences, therapy does not typically move to a rosier place. Increased growth often brings with it an increased sense of loss. We understand that, developmentally, each stage of growth means leaving behind a Self, a way of being, that involves genuine loss. In fact, at times one may feel that if a client does not experience that sense of loss, the gains may only be intellectually achieved and the true work of experiencing lies ahead. And so we understand the parent's grief at seeing children go off to college, or getting married, not as pathology, but as a genuine acknowledgment that an era is ending, ending forever. And that because the changes may be constructive, because this constitutes "growth," it in no way diminishes the real and pained loss.

A client struggling for many years to think more of his own needs, rather than orienting himself primarily to those of others, came in the course of therapy to be quite successful in his business ventures. He found himself imagining that if his mother came to his recently opened branch office, rather than sharing his delight, she would seem disappointed. This added to his feelings that gaining something for himself, being successful, would not bring something good, but only ultimate disappointment and isolation. As we explored, through fantasy, his mother's reactions, a touching story emerged. She did not turn out to be simply a competitive or envious woman (in his fantasies). What emerged was a woman who had known a certain role in relationship to her son. She knew how to give advice or to make suggestions if he were feeling inadequate or unsure of himself. It was a role both felt comfortable with. But if he became a successful businessman the only role she then knew would be lost. And he imagined her feeling lost and anxious, fearful that no new role would emerge. As he thought about her dilemma he began to cry. It was clear that it was not his mother he was simply talking about, but his identification with his mother. His new-won achievements carried with them the grief of giving up a flawed but familiar way of relating, a way that was quintessentially familiar to him. Gains could not be met without loss. So each client who changes must face this kind of loss. And for many people who prematurely drop out of treatment, there is a fear that any future gains will in no way measure up to the anticipated loss. The therapist who ignores this, is insensitive to this, avoids his own grief, may subtly or not so subtly support such termination.

Too little appreciation goes into the enormous effort that clients put into developing the "Self" that they bring to therapy. Even if that Self is to *not have* a Self (what we frequently experience in our work with borderline patients), or the Self is the most abusing and abusive, or abrasive or withdrawn or seemingly impossibly defended against (as we see in psychotic patients) there is an enormous attachment to that very Self. Thus when a woman who was quite paranoid, and depressed enough to be hospitalized and receive shock therapy, began to emerge from that prison of the soul, it was not with warmth and openness, but rather with a tremendous amount of grief. Her grief was manyfold. It was the grief of giving up some enormously important identifications with her family. It was the grief of letting in an enormous amount of unhappiness that had been defended against. It was the grief of facing a lifetime of hurt and pain, hidden till then behind an angry, accusing, belligerent presence. And the therapist, while certainly welcoming this enormous change, felt himself not happy, but similarly depressed with the years spent with her in struggle, and the attachment that he had formed to that abrasive person who was now leaving.

Patients who make major personality changes frequently have dreams in which a person is dying (a part of themselves), or in which an infant is dying (a fetal Self that cannot mature, but must be grieved). And often the therapist feels a kind of helplessness within himself or herself, which may parallel the feelings of a parent who has lost a child. It is both a real feeling, for something is truly being lost, and it may be a transference-induced feeling, as one experiences the feelings that the patient's parents could not let themselves experience. Sometimes it is the awareness of the therapist's own personal losses as a child that either surface anew or for the first time in truly profound psychotherapy.

And often one fears at this moment that the patient will break off the therapy—a fear which is both real and projective. No therapist gets to do all the grief work he or she needs to do. And so there is always some part of the therapist that does not want to do the grief work either. And patients know this, even when we may hide it from ourselves.

In this paper I have tried to give some flavor of how I think of issues of commitment as they occur in the psychotherapy relationship. I have tried to indicate that whether the patient stays in therapy or leaves involves a subtle interplay or forces within the patient, between the patient and therapist. There is subtle interplay of anxieties that get played out in the relationship. And finally there is a struggle with the therapist and his or her own sense of Self. Both therapist and patient struggle with similar issues and similar anxieties. I have tried to focus on some of these anxieties as they emerge in the therapy relationship. How these get played out is unique to each therapist and each client, and each unique therapy relationship.

Comment

Dr. Tirnauer poses the issue of commitment as representing a problem of choice. Within the context of psychotherapy, the decision to make or not make a commitment involves conflict between the wish to change and the anxieties which inevitably result and which serve as a resistance to change. His paper focuses on three common resistances: the fear of loss of control, the fear of intimacy, and the fear of loss (of one's old sense of self, of important relationships). The list of issues could easily be extended, and they vary for each patient.

But whatever the risks are, I view the therapeutic task as one of increasing the patient's capacity for commitment. This seems to me to involve three principal components: namely, the ability to tolerate anxiety, self-esteem, and autonomy. Let me discuss each briefly in turn.

In normal development, the good parent protects the child from traumatic anxiety and excessive stimulation. The parent reassures the child when he or she becomes anxious and teaches the child how to soothe itself. The parent's acceptance of the total person of the child (i.e., drives, feelings, behavior, ego strengths and limitations, etc.) is conveyed through empathic mirroring, helping the child to internalize a realistic, stable, and positively-valued sense of self. This structualization fosters the development of higher level defenses for coping with anxiety.

A second requirement for making commitments is self-esteem. Patients who felt unwanted, a nuisance, or a disappointment often find it difficult to make an investment in others or in themselves because no significant person had made an investment in them. The therapist's own positive self-esteem, commitment to personal growth, and genuine positive regard for the patient may hopefully be internalized by the patient, thus fostering greater capacity for commitment to the therapeutic process.

A third element in the capacity for commitment is a sense of oneself as a separate, independent person (i.e., object constancy). For me to make a commitment to you, and to feel I have a choice in the matter, I need to see you as a separate person with your own needs and feelings. If this is absent, the patient is likely to pull away from commitment out of a fear of being engulfed. Commitment means saying "yes." If a patient has not achieved individuation, it is because the parent did not respect that patient's "no" when he or she was a child. These patients now feel a need to insist upon their "no" in order to feel separate. Consequently they cannot truly say "yes." A primary task we have as therapists is to support the autonomy of our patients. Otherwise, all of their energy will go into opposing us or, alternatively, they will become so dependent they will be unable to leave. In neither case is their capacity for commitment being enhanced.

A brief clinical example may make these issues more clear. A young woman came for help in mourning the loss of an important family member. Clinical assessment revealed that she rigidly controlled all of her feelings and was very intellectual. She was afraid that mourning would cause her to go crazy (i.e., to become so depressed that she would never recover). Further investigation revealed a history of child abuse, a loss of appropriate parenting which also threatened her with terrifying rage. It was thus understandable why she had dropped out of treatment with previous therapists, who pressed her to "feel"—her stated treatment goal, but one which she was not yet strong enough to handle. What was needed instead was support in "*not* feeling," at least until she had developed confidence in being able to shut off excessive feelings. Her distrust of the therapist needed to be supported rather than challenged. Only after a year of intensive work along these lines was she ready to begin experiencing her feelings about smaller, current losses in her life and even then they threatened her so much at times that her ego functioning would regress for brief periods. As she experienced herself as being stronger, with better defenses, she became more able to commit herself to experiencing her feelings rather than "putting them on the shelf."

In summary, I view the therapeutic task as one of assessing the patient's ego functioning and working to strengthen the patient in ego terms (defenses, self-esteem, autonomy). Paradoxically, this may require the therapist initially to give understanding and support to the patient's reluctance to make commitments (as the case example illustrated). In the long run, however, as the patient is assisted in the task of separation/individuation, the capacity for commitment will grow. This will also increase the probability that the patient will choose to make a commitment to personal growth.

Gordon F. Boals, PhD

The Many Faces of the Hesitant Patient

Robert J. Willis

Heat shouted against Covenant's face like the voice of his destiny; but he did not stop. He could not stop. Entranced and compelled, he rode the mourning of the Sea forward.

Into the fire.

. . . . . .

Burning, he opened himself to the surrounding flames.

They rushed to incinerate him; but he was ready. He mastered the fire with argence, bent it to his command. Flame and power were projected outward together, so that the blaze lashed tremendously into the night.

He spread his arms to the city, stretched himself as if he yearned to embrace the whole of The Grieve.

In wild magic, white puissance without sound, he shouted: Come! This is the *caamora!* Come and be healed!

Stephen Donaldson, *The Wounded Land*

For anyone who has experienced psychotherapy, at times the call to health has much of the mixed attractiveness that this science fiction hero's had for the shades of his giant friends! No matter the promise of *eventual* happiness; the medicine sometimes seems to surpass the illness in its ability to produce *present pain.*

Facing the dilemma of personal pain within and therapeutic pain outside, quite understandably a patient often hesitates. "Where, really, may I find a good option? My choice appears to lie only in the lesser of two very distasteful realities." To the attending therapist, that hesitation may look like a lack of commitment. And sometimes that may be true. As we in this paper consider the many faces of the hesitant patient, we ought in justice, however, to keep in mind the question: hesitation concerning

Robert J. Willis, Ph.D., a diplomate in counseling psychology with specialties in psychotherapy and religious psychology, lives in Ewing Township, NJ.

what and for what reasons? Caution and fairness require that we search for understanding within the life of each person. After all, therapy is a journey undertaken for one's own self, not for the sake of therapy or therapist.

Of primary importance to this topic is the distinction among the resistant, reluctant, and uncommitted patient or client. All in a generic sense may be judged "hesitant," but the hesitation in each specific case comes out of very different personal stances.

Because this special issue is devoted to the topic of the uncommitted *patient,* that term, one which comes out of a tradition of psychopathology, will be employed when speaking of a lack of commitment or when discussing the psychodynamic concept of the resistant patient. *Client,* a term in favor among therapists coming out of a growth concept of counseling, will be used when referring to reluctance.

THE RESISTANT PATIENT

To anyone familiar with the psychodynamic tradition, the concept of resistance seems commonplace. And, as Fritz Redl (1966) remarks, any good psychotherapist, no matter the philosophical persuasion, meets it constantly: "Resistance is an unavoidable process in every effective treatment, for that part of the personality that has an interest in the survival of the pathology actively protests each time therapy comes close to producing change" (p. 216).

In the course of human life, each of us knows personal need, the insensitivity of others, the urgent requirement to protect oneself from the inevitable threats and pains of the human condition. What do we do? We build walls—indeed, a fortress—to keep the instruments of pain outside and a sense of personal safety and well being within. Everyone, prudently, has such a protected place.

Sadly, however, some people fashion for themselves a prison instead. A fortress is fine in the face of an attacking enemy, but what if, when the attacker withdraws and a friend beckons, one discovers that no gates have been built into these fortified walls? or no key can open those locked doors? or rusting hinges have welded shut all means of exit? What once protected, now isolates; what once warded off pain, now increases the searing fires of loneliness.

Confronted with these walls and the personal paralysis that freezes them closed, a therapist has many options:

1. Pretend, at least for the moment, that they don't exist. In this way the pain will not now be increased, and resistance for a time will be avoided.

2. Call attention to their existence by knocking softly at the gates. The patient may then choose not to hear, thus avoiding additional pain; may hear but protest that nothing can help to open them, thus avoiding the pain of change; may respond only with a cry for help, thus refusing to accept personal responsibility for taking action which might be painful. In every instance, resistance reigns.
3. Launch an all-out attack on the gates. Should the patient strive to ward off this assault as being in effect no different from that of any enemy, again resistance results.

From this metaphoric explanation, we may see that resistance is built up by three things: the patient's history of protection in the face of perceived threat, the therapist's method of confronting a protection turned self-destructive, and the patient's response to the therapist's challenging of these still-protective though confining defenses. Resistance, no matter its specific content, arises out of the interaction between a patient who both loves and hates the self-imposed defensive restrictions and a therapist who must constantly search for the best way of helping the patient get control over them. Resistance may result from an ill-advised or inappropriate or poorly timed confrontation of the patient's defenses; it may also be the expected response to an appropriate call to change and, indeed, may be its necessary precursor.

By way of concluding this discussion of the resistant patient, a case example may help concretize this quite common resistance to change.

A young, overweight woman patient arrives 10 minutes late for her therapy session. Traffic problems! But she also announces that her usual pleasant anticipation of her therapy hour is missing; indeed, on the drive over she twice thought of turning around, or canceling her appointment. Why? A mystery!

She also had a recent aggravating dream to report. Alone in an antebellum mansion, she had walked up a magnificent marble staircase only to find the door at the top locked. Try as she might, she couldn't open it. She awoke, frustrated. What did the room conceal? Why the stubborn lock?

Using guided imagery, she revisited this dream mansion. All went well until she again approached the offending door. Still locked! Suggestions to look for keys hanging from nails or for axes leaning ready in corners produced nothing. Only the suggestion that she might, like Alice, become very small and thus slip under the door gave immediate entrance to a large, well-furnished but unoccupied sitting room.

Through French doors, also locked, she could see a lovely, alluring garden. "I must visit it!" But she couldn't open the doors, nor would she be willing to leave them open if she could get into the garden. Being out there must be securely private.

The suggestion of a secret button, one known only to her, finally al-

lowed her to spring the locks, enter the garden, and close the doors behind her.

For the next few minutes she explored this gorgeous place, and in the
process found herself being transformed into a beautiful woman.

Fantasy ended, eyes glistening, she exclaimed: "I *am* beautiful! I've
never been able to admit that, especially to myself."

The hesitance about this session and the late arrival, the frustrating
dream and unyielding door, no available key or axe, the locked garden:
all resistances to change, yet all heralds of her soon-to-be-cherished beauty.

✕ *THE RELUCTANT CLIENT*

However strenuously the resistant patient may hang on to frozen defenses, at least that person has voluntarily chosen to be in the therapeutic
relationship. Not so the reluctant client. "Reluctance, as herein understood, refers to unvoluntariness—to the prospective client's not wanting
to be a client in the first place" (Vriend & Dyer, 1973, p. 240). And as
the authors (Riordan, Matheny, & Harris, 1978) of "Helping Counselors
Minimize Client Reluctance" so sharply point out, "counseling literature
and courses almost always assume that clients are self-selected and self-
referred. In reality, however, most counselors work with large numbers
of reluctant and unmotivated clients" (p. 6).

The reluctant client often acts like the resistant patient. Both keep silent, nod or shrug when questioned; both respond hostilely and defensively, or reveal only what is expected; both seek to avoid, to keep the focus
off of self, to maintain defenses by sharing only low priority items
(Vriend & Dyer, 1973, p. 241). But the actions of the reluctant client may
be attributed to much different reasons.

Many clients sit in the therapist's office because they must. Civil courts
often demand treatment; harassed and frantic parents often drag unwilling
youngsters with them into family therapy; in the face of a divorce ultima-
tum, a reluctant spouse often follows an aggrieved mate into marital therapy. Sometimes no option to attendance in therapy exists; sometimes
therapy simply constitutes a reprieve from something worse. In either situation, attendance is compulsory, feels coercive, and is perceived as a
violation of one's personal integrity. Who, indeed, wouldn't be reluctant
in such a situation!

Given the forced attendance, the reluctance flows out of specific attitudes and circumstances. For some "a mind set of reluctance will dis-
prove the notion that the person responsible for the client being in the
counseling setting was, in fact, correct"; for others "the act of being
nonconformist or uncooperative is an avenue for acceptance in certain

circles'' (Vriend & Dyer, 1973, p. 241). And "some reluctant clients have negative attitudes toward counseling because they are waging a constant skirmish with the system" (p. 242). In every instance, the reluctance, though acted out vis-à-vis the therapist, has little to do with the therapist or the particular therapeutic situation. Rather, its focus is outside the therapist's office; the message is sent, not to the therapist, but to important others in the client's life.

Of course, the reasons for reluctance may also include the therapeutic situation. For some, to enter at all into the therapy would be to accept the possibility of need or to admit the unacceptable possibility of personal inadequacy. For others, therapy is seen quite clearly to be an assault upon one's well being, as an unwarranted and illegitimate and unwanted demand to open oneself to another. "I don't need therapy, but even if I did, I wouldn't be in therapy because someone forced me to be, and besides, I wouldn't be in therapy with you!"

Where resistance may be attributed to the ongoing process of therapy and to the movement of the therapeutic interaction, reluctance pre-dates the meeting of therapist and client. And its acting out has little to do with either the content or the process of the meeting in the therapist's office.

This is not to say that the psychotherapist has no responsibility to work with the reluctant client, or that no effective strategies for doing so exist. The responsibilities and strategies, however, differ from those that resistance occasions.

Recognizing the validity of the complaint that literature about client reluctance is "leaning heavily on inspiration and falling short of systematizing what we know regarding human behavior" (Riordan, Matheny, & Harris, 1978, p. 7), something should be said here about effective strategies in working with the reluctant client.

As reported by Riordan, Matheny, and Harris, different writers counsel different strategies. Fleisher (1972) urges "the counselor to be 'active, involved and direct' and to possess a strong personal value system that is clearly visible but to behave in a nonauthoritative manner" (p. 69). Krainen (1972), interpreting the reluctant behavior as manipulative, quite directly calls for the therapist to engage in countermanipulation. Glasser (1965) in *Reality Therapy* recommends "the clarification and acceptance of responsibilities by the client. Vriend and Dyer suggest direct confrontation of reluctance in the client. Riordan, Matheny, and Harris speak at some length to the behavioral strategies which may turn the lack of motivation of the reluctant patient into motivation.

Including, yet expanding upon, strategies offered by Vriend and Dyer, (1973) this writer has found most effective the following:

1. Recognize that the reluctance is not directed at oneself but to a situation that feels coercive.

2. Recognize one's own negative reactions to the reluctance, accept their validity, and the validity of the reluctance.
3. Deal openly with the reluctance—its presence and validity, one's acceptance of it, and the willingness to work with it.
4. Separate in one's own mind behavior that (a) may be attributed to the reluctant state, (b) is a reflection of typical ways of acting, (c) results from the uniqueness of this relationship, and (d) comes from the therapeutic resistance.
5. Reframe for oneself and for the client the negative reluctance into the positive desire for personal freedom and integrity.
6. Help the client explore the reasons for the reluctance, taking special note of and calling attention to the client's strength and openness in dealing with the reluctance.
7. Seek to understand the context outside therapy that the reluctance is primarily addressing.
8. Separate oneself openly from any desire to, or any activity which in fact does, coerce the client.
9. Expand the client's way of understanding the situation by supporting other ways of looking at it.
10. Note, reinforce, and work in areas where the client shows flexibility and the possibility of therapeutic movement.

A wife recently made an appointment for marital therapy. In the first moment of meeting her and her husband it was evident by his glum, un-smiling "hello" that he would, to echo W.C. Fields, rather be dead than in this place for exploring marital discord! A subsequent noting of his hostile mood revealed that his attendance simply forestalled a threatened divorce: "Come or else."

Given this coercion, no wonder his reluctance! This I reflected to him, at the same time commenting how his hostility may well be signaling his desire to respect himself by taking responsibility for his own decisions and resultant actions. The gloom lifted ever so little. With the suggestion that there were probably many reasons for not wanting to be here, with gathering interest he began to share his sense of betrayal over her "suddenly seeing things wrong with us and our marriage after all these years." With the comment that the marriage had always seemed just fine to him and showed, from his perspective, no need for change, he allowed that "I would like to see a few things different, mind you." By the time we had explored some of those possible changes, he was speaking almost forcefully and with animation: "Just maybe we could get rid of some dog-gone things that have bugged me for years!"

By the end of the session both wife *and* husband had agreed for next time to list separately desired changes and to describe their secret ideal of a perfect life together.

By allowing this reluctant man to be who he truly was—reluctant, by understanding his hostility as no reflection upon the therapist, by exploring with him how he might act appropriately in his reluctant state, and by following up on his own desire for change, this therapist was able to help a very reluctant person decide for himself that being a therapy client might not be so bad after all!

THE UNCOMMITTED PATIENT

A literature review undertaken specifically for this paper turned up many writings concerned with resistant patients and reluctant clients, but absolutely nothing about the uncommitted. This lack simply reinforces this writer's experience that in 20 years of work in psychology, he has never heard the topic so much as mentioned in lecture or class, seminar or workshop, professional journal or professional conversation. The following discussion, therefore, necessarily is drawn out of the actual experiences of working with patients who were in some fashion "uncommitted."

Keeping in mind the definitions given of the resistant patients and reluctant clients, we may describe the uncommitted patient this way: When the patient's motivations for being in therapy are incompatible with the therapeutic context, incongruent with the therapist's motivations, or unacceptable to the therapist, the patient will then be perceived by the therapist as uncommitted. Voluntarily entering the therapeutic context, this patient is not a reluctant client. Refusing to go where the therapist beckons, this patient's refusal is caused by a motivational structure that differs appreciably from that of the therapist. This patient, therefore, though acting simiarly to the resistant patient, is really uncommitted.

At least five faces of noncommitment may be identified. Let us consider each in turn.

1. Contact Only

Some patients find their way into a therapist's office for reasons totally foreign to the therapeutic process. A man, for example, comes for therapy because his wife had entered therapy, was finding it very helpful and thought that he might also. Although he is quite happy and content with his life, although he has no specific problems that he cannot handle, although he has no particular desire to be any different than he is, to please her he makes an appointment. After one rules out any undue dependency on his part, his state may be judged to be one of noncommitment to the work of therapy.

A young woman, panicked, seeks therapy. A working diagnosis suggests schizophrenia. Over the course of four sessions it becomes evident that she does not want to use the therapy to rid herself of the pathology; rather, she wants it reinforced and strengthened. Her panic is coming, not from the psychosis, but from the fear that the realities of daily life might succeed in making her hurt enough to dare working against the schizophrenic protections. In these short weeks, the panic quiets, the fear lessens, and she is content to remain in her schizophrenic state. Relative to therapy, she is uncommitted.

Successful therapy appears to depend on a patient state of hurting or yearning. Each person has a threshold, a level of hurting or yearning *enough,* that must be crossed for a commitment to the change goals of therapy to be made. When absent, the person has not, in effect, the necessary components for daring the therapeutic process.

2. *No Therapeutic Relationship*

On occasion, a person comes for therapy who does have problems, who would like to be different, but who is using the therapy for reasons foreign to it. Consider the following:

It's California in the mid-1960s. A middle-aged man, an ex-Green Beret, desires therapy ostensibly because of marital difficulties. From his opening sally, ''I hear you're a non-directive therapist,'' it's clear that he has one main desire: to be in control of the therapeutic situation. Thus begins a struggle of some weeks' duration. It ended with this declaration: ''You know, I truly came here only for one reason: to have a therapist like all my friends do. A status symbol, you know. I've enjoyed our sessions, you have been helpful, and I'm even beginning to like you. But now it's becoming more difficult not to enter into this—really. I probably could use therapy, and maybe I'll come back for it someday, but I don't want it now. Thank you.''

A recent high-school graduate gets fired from a managerial trainee position, doesn't get the support and sympathy he wants from his pediatrician father, so in a rage he makes superficial cuts on his arms and legs. Frantic, the father seeks psychiatric and psychological aid for his son. Within four weeks, as the shifted responsibility lessens Dad's panic, pills are not being taken and therapy sessions are being missed or tardily attended. It becomes increasingly clear that the patient prefers his agitated and disturbed state to a healthier, happier one in which he cannot command his father's presence and concern. Through his actions he steadfastly and effectively refuses to enter into a therapeutic alliance with the therapist because to do such would be to give up his real reason for coming for therapy: the manipulation of a distant father. His commitment was there, but not to the therapy.

3. *Symptoms Only*

Quite frequently, patients seek therapeutic assistance for a very specific reason: to get rid of some disturbing thing in their life. They do not desire to use the therapeutic occasion to get at the causes of the particular disturbance, nor even to prevent its reoccurrence. Immediate relief for them signals the completion of a successful therapy.

Consider a rather dramatic example. In terror a 23-year-old man begs for an appointment. He is being assaulted by the spirits of two long-deceased uncles, both of whom, in life, he disliked.

During his first session he describes their voices constantly demanding he do things he hates, their materializing near him (when he concentrates and generally in darkened rooms), their threats of dire consequences should he try to get rid of them.

His immediate disturbance is judged to be attributed to three possible things: (1) evil spirits, (2) a psychotic attack, (3) an overactive imagination. What is most evident, however, is his out-of-control state. Whatever else, personal control must be reasserted as a natural requirement for commencing therapy.

In no uncertain terms the therapist tells him the following:

1. Theologically, a good God will not tempt a person past his ability and will not allow spirits to take over a person's will.
2. Psychologically, we know that we do not perceive things as they are in themselves outside us, that our minds put together our sense impressions in a usual and recognizable way. And, moreover, perceptual distortions may be caused by intense attention.
3. Behaviorally, a way of removing an obsession is to stop paying attention to it immediately and to move one's attention to something both pleasant and healthful.

Given the above, he leaves with the following strategy: When they next appear, he is to tell these spirits to "go to Hell" because his therapist, at least, isn't afraid of them; he is not to listen to them or try to see them; he is straightway to do something he enjoys. His next appointment will be in 4 days.

The 4 days pass. He calls to cancel his appointment. The spirits left after his first post-session encounter with them! He is delighted with the therapy, quite grateful, and he will certainly call on the therapist again if he ever has any other problems!

What was wrong with him? Will the problem reoccur? The therapist can only guess because his patient was not committed to therapy any further than removing the immediate symptom.

4. Conflicting Priorities

A lack of commitment to therapy at times may be traced to its being relegated to a minority position in a person's life. Therapy is desired, problems need addressing, change would be most welcome, but other demands in one's life are more pressing.

A couple is concerned about a teenage son, the third of seven children. The family lives on a small farm, the father owns a construction company, the mother works as an executive secretary in a small corporation. The boy is having problems at school: falling grades, fights, general unhappiness. At home he is irritable and distant. The parents seek therapeutic guidance.

After two sessions—widely spread and after numerous cancellations—it becomes evident that serious problems exist in the marriage, not the least of which is absence occasioned by overwhelming schedules. Marital therapy is suggested, agreed upon, and scheduled.

Six weeks and one full/one half session later, therapy is discontinued. The couple will not make the necessary adjustments in their lives that will allow any time together, not even a consistent hour of therapy per week. They are not resistant patients—no therapeutic movement has had a chance to start. They are not reluctant clients—both truly desire the therapy. They are uncommitted patients—their life motivations and set priorities simply block successful entrance into therapy. In effect they would rather accept the painful status quo than make shifts necessary for a committed therapeutic endeavor.

5. Single-Stage Commitment

What signals the completion of therapy? One patient leaves therapy over the therapist's complaint: "But we still haven't found the cause." Another patient stops even though the therapist counsels that "there is still much to do." And another informs her therapist that "if I go on, I will move into material that will take years to deal with; at this time, I am not ready to make that commitment."

In each instance, the patients desire to go only so far in therapy, and their assessment of how far that should be differs from the therapist's goal. For them the therapy has helped them move to a particular level of happiness and health. More could be done. They don't deny this. But more will not be done, at least not now.

At this juncture, a therapist may treat this desire to quit as resistance. Sometimes it is. In some instances, however, it merely reflects the patient's decision to be committed to therapy only up to a given point. Any problem here often becomes the therapist's: I must swallow *my* disappointment, let go of *my* goals for the patient, and allow the person to go on with *his or her* life—without me!

In dealing with the uncommitted patient, the following strategies are useful:

1. Distinguish clearly among resistance, reluctance, and lack of commitment.
2. Assess the real and controlling reasons that led the patient into therapy.
3. Be aware of one's own goals for the patient, especially if they appear to differ appreciably from the patient's goals.
4. Recognize that a lack of commitment to the therapist's goals does not reflect on the therapist but rather is the expression of the patient's life that is larger than the therapeutic relationship.
5. In the face of a cessation of therapeutic movement, confront openly any perceived lack of commitment.
6. Help the patient weigh the commitment to therapy against the other commitments in the patient's life.
7. Support the patient in the decision-making process, whether it means the continuation or the cessation of therapy.
8. Separate one's own goals and feelings relative to the continuation of therapy from those of the patient.
9. Recognize with the patient that a "satisfactory" therapy does not necessarily mean a "complete" one in some objective and absolute sense.
10. Hold open the possibility of a resumption of therapy at some later date should priorities and commitments in the patient's life shift.

CONCLUSION

Think back for a moment to the intriguing, or at least different, selection from *The Wounded Land* (Donaldson, 1980, p. 484) which introduced this discussion. In the light of what has been now presented, listen to the following parallel development of that passage. It may serve as a link between the science fiction story and the story of therapy. It may also serve as a summary conclusion.

Thomas Covenant (the therapist) has placed himself in front of "The Grieve," the place where the giants wrestled with death (the therapeutic struggle with separation and division). In order to assist those tortured shades (people struggling in spirit), he must do three things: (1) be willing to confront the evil that killed them (face the psychological state); (2) be passionate in that confrontation (bring the force of one's living psyche to bear on the inner division); (3) be willing to control the raging fire as being the place of *their* purification (accept the therapy as their responsibility).

The dead giants must come into the fire willingly (not as reluctant clients), even though the pain may make them recoil (resistance is inevitable). The fire will not destroy them, only purify them of their guilt (each therapy, as each life, is unique). Out of his love for them, Thomas offers them the chance to be free (to be healed and to grow), each according to his or her own need (to the level of, and according to, each one's commitment).

The giants enter the purifying flames because they trust Thomas's power (the therapist's life, training, and experience). He has braved the flames (willingly deals with psychological problems). They also trust their own life experiences of other painful yet nondestructive *caamora* (patients trust their own life struggle).

According to the level of a patient's hesitation then, and recognizing the many faces that appear to be commitment or its absence, may we, with Thomas, be ready to shout: "Come and be healed!"

Comment

I grew up in a family heavily infused with the medical essence. With both parents professionally involved with medicine, one a physician and the other a nurse, I found the medical subculture to permeate my life rather thoroughly. As a young child I spent interminable hours in the interns' quarters on those weekends when both parents were working—one "on duty," the other interning. Later in my childhood I lived in the center of the medical activity of my small home town, my parents' office being in our house for several years. So, I grew up hearing medical talk at home and at parties. Being a child, I was allowed behind the scenes, where I was privy not only to the talk, but to the medical activities. I saw the apparatus and from time to time the medical procedures when there was something especially interesting such as a gunshot wound to be dressed or an exposed tendon to be tucked back and sewn away from view. Only after being away from this subculture for years have I been able to look back and assess its impact on my formation, and to gain a perspective as an informed outsider. One insight I have gained is extremely important to me. *Physicians are less afraid of treating their patients than patients are of receiving treatment.* This I declare to be the first axiom of interpersonal medical dynamics.

How easily the surgeon can recommend the scalpel! To "surgeon" one needs patients. If what one knows how to do is to "surgeon," then one tends to get reasonably comfortable doing that after many trials. Two factors are pertinent here in differentiating the experience of the surgeon from that of the patient. First, the surgeon, in most cases, is very familiar with the procedure and the setting. He or she is at home with the sights, the sounds, and the smells of surgery, as well as with the activity itself. To the patient, this scene is of another subculture, known about, but not known. Second, and obviously, the surgeon does the procedure, the patient receives. There is a "cutter" and a "cuttee," with the latter being the one who is physically invaded, whose life is at risk, and who will bear the physical pain of the aftermath.

I have presented this background and this axiom in order to suggest an analogy. The axiom applies equally well to the enactment of psychotherapy. To wit, *psychotherapists are less afraid of doing psychotherapy than patients are of receiving it.* This axiom is too easily overlooked. Those of us who belong to the psychotherapy subculture are often so ensconced in it that we fail to appreciate how threatening it can be to the outsider.

Willis' distinction of the resistant, the reluctant, and the uncommitted patient strikes me as an important one. In each case the patient may hesitate to enter fully and wholeheartedly into therapy, into that realm where we therapists feel at home. Willis reported finding nothing in the literature concerning the uncommitted patient, and this makes his distinction of that category of particular importance. I like his elaboration of "five faces of noncommitment." In reading these I came to a corollary of the above-stated axiom: *Psychotherapy patients do not necessarily want what the psychotherapist would prefer to offer.*

From our perspective, within the psychotherapy subculture, we may envision possibilities which are foreign to, or beyond what the patient is able to see. And, *we* may have little or no fear of sallying forth toward such ends. When this discrepancy arises, a stance which is respectful of the patient is certainly in order. The strategies for dealing with the "uncommitted" patient which Willis offers impress me as being highly respectful. Surely, patients have the right to limit their commitment to that process where it is we who are at home.

Edward W. L. Smith, Ph.D.

The Fear of Commitment to Life

Richard F. Formica

At a recent conference a colleague described to me a rather unusual scene. He went to study with Milton Erickson, noted hypnotherapist, for a week. Erickson greeted each person who had gathered in his conference room with a handshake. But the handshake with each person was invariably longer and at a different tempo than the recipient expected. By the time Milton Erickson began one of his famous "therapeutic stories" most of the participants, who were all highly trained psychotherapists, were in a mild trance state. Erickson had so disrupted their expectations, in a gentle, non-obtrusive way, that their old mind-sets were cleared and the participants were available for new experience. Let's set aside our own preconceived ideas about commitment and the uncommitted patient and take a journey together.

We see patients who are frightened of commitment to intimate love relations, of commitment to career pursuits, of commitment to success, of commitment to fathering, of commitment to joy and happiness. At the core, all patients are terrified of commitment to life. All patients frantically avoid commitment to full and direct and immediate experience. Patients differ in the specific aspects of life which scare them and in the almost infinite variety of ways they have evolved to avoid life in its bald essence. But they all shrink back in the face of the *mysterium tremendum* which is direct, uncensored, unmitigated experience of life and self with no compromising defenses. But please, let's not knock the "uncommitted" patient, for that is the name of the game. Patients cannot help being uncommitted in their essence. It is their very fright of living experience that drives them to our offices. They ask for our understanding and patience.

Beyond this, all *therapists* are essentially uncommitted. By this I am not referring to the bored or jaded therapists, the dilettante, or the manipulative entrepreneur. I am speaking of me and you who spend hours thinking about our patients, reading books and journals, seeking therapy and supervision for ourselves and our work. Yet, at the core we are uncommitted. In our past there were experiences which were too powerful

Richard F. Formica, Ph.D., is a psychologist in Teaneck, NJ, practicing a blend of creative analytic humanism. He is cofounder of the Bergen County Parent Workshop program, and the Interpersonal Skills Institute.

to deal with, too traumatizing and immobilizing. And so we also need healing as persons and as therapists. Yet we too still shrink back from full, uncompromised experience. Our tears do not freely and frequently spill over as we listen to human tragedy. We soften the blow of tragic or maddening experience by processing the "patient" through the conceptualizations of our theories and the distanced safety of our techniques. So, to our patience and understanding with our uncommitted patients, we might add humility, for we add our own compromise with life to the therapeutic interaction. We are made of the same flesh and blood.

Perhaps I might now present yet another idea in this evolving journey of ours. By looking from just a slightly different angle, I can readily observe that all of us, patients, therapists, writers, and readers are thoroughly committed. Patients are committed deeply to their private illusions, such as, "I can't do it," "Mother owes me," "I can't live without him." Therapists are also committed to their own professionally shared illusions by which they say, "I know the truth. Live like me and you will be happier." Much therapy is actually the therapist inducing the patient to trade his neurotic, suffering-producing illusions for the therapist's consensually validated, change-producing illusions. Much good comes of this exchange. The patient has a new way to approach life, new glasses from behind which he views life; the therapist is confirmed in a positive approach to life and its sufferings. But the radical commitment to live directly, here and now, with each other in the face of the mysterium tremendum of life is often bypassed in much of our therapies. We shelter our selves and our patients from this experience by our mutually shared and supported commitment to live through illusion, even healthy illusion.

In fact, we would rather die than face life with complete vulnerability, stripped totally of all protective mechanisms, soothing theories, beliefs, and platitudes. We would rather die—that is, not live fully, avoid experience, anesthetize ourselves—than face the awfulness of death, with its terror, pain, unknownness, and the possibility of total annihilation. It is any wonder that patients fear therapy and fear commitment to its challenge? We ask them to live fully, whereas their entire life has been spent avoiding just this. We ask them to die to their known way of living, to surrender their self-protective ways of thinking, believing, acting, and feeling in exchange for the void we call "possibility." And they say, as do we in our own lives, "No way!" The awful immediacy of experience is too much for most of us most of the time. The glare of reality is too blinding. But they and we try anyway and, miraculously, we succeed often in inching our way along this mysterious and frightening path of life.

And it is *urgent* to follow this path, to die and to be reborn, to create a kingdom of life within. The only pathway to joy is to surrender our cherished illusions and *to experience this precious gift of life just as it is given to us.* Yet who can blame a patient for not wishing to pursue this demanding and relentless challenge. The therapist may think he or she is only asking a small thing, like "give up an unhappy marriage" or "learn to speak in public" but the patient is wiser. The patient knows you are asking him or her to die and trust in rebirth. No small request!

And so it is with each and every one of our patients, not just the obviously, stereotypically uncommitted ones. Some get frightened and show their "uncommittedness" by frequently missing meetings. Others by not taking the possibility of change seriously. Others protect themselves by refusing to attach themselves to us in a human way, treating us as interchangeable dispensing machines. Others are more subtle. They display their terrors by eagerly free-associating to everything in sight, never once slowing down long enough to look at us and say, quietly and deeply, "I love you. Thank you for listening." And we collude, because we too are more comfortable with analysis or behavior reprogramming than with the reality of life experienced directly. We get annoyed if the patient's style of uncommitment is inconvenient or unflattering, but so often we let true uncommitment—the failure to experience life directly in intimate relation—pass us by.

Once, after one of the most powerful therapeutic experiences I had ever undergone, I felt reality directly in all its naked power and beauty. I could do nothing but stare, enchanted. For 3 days colors were intensely brighter; music was full and moving; time floated. My body was softer. Shoulders fell and arms felt longer. I was totally open to the patients I worked with during those 3 days. I simply received them. Cried with them. Laughed with them. I stayed with them in the full immediacy of their experience without intervening barriers. And they were very open to me in a surprisingly reciprocal way. Even my most uncommitted paranoid patient said to me, "My God, what was with you yesterday? You were so open it was contagious!" And yet I was terrified. Everything I knew and clung to was dying, falling away. After 3 days, I ran back to "normal" reality so that I could get back to the familiar and "important" business of opening my mail and paying my bills. Safety at last!

Patients are a lot like the "me" that I've described above. We all want to live fully. We all want to be courageous. We all are frightened to enter the unknown. We courageously change and then run back to safety. Commitment to life and uncommitment to life wage an endless battle, with terror and courage pitted against each other to the death.

Psychotherapy intends to give sight to patients. To offer them new life, new opportunity. Why, you may still ask, are patients so often uncommitted to therapy in general, and to change in particular? Recent studies of men and women born blind because of cataracts to whom sight was restored when they were in their 20s or 30s or 40s has revealed something most interesting: Though all these adults were thoroughly familiar with their worlds, they were completely overwhelmed and terrified when their sight was restored! Life in its raw, undigested form was too much for them. Many asked to have their sight removed again and, for all, it took weeks and months to feel safe and comfortable again. So when we cast about for theories about why patients fear the "simple" experience of Reality as it is, let's not forget the trauma of these previously blind men and women. The only reason we can't really understand our patients' terror and uncommittedness is that the personal and cultural myths by which we ourselves have tamed Reality simply work too well. We are now too smug in our feeling that life is very simple and there is nothing to fear.

I would like to end this article on a personal note. The piece of therapeutic work which engrosses me now is coming face to face with the reality of death. Death—the annihilation of self as I know me; the loss of relatedness to loved ones as I know relatedness; the final triumph of reality over my defenses, illusions, and myths. Regardless of what I think death is and regardless of what I want death to be, it stands before me in shrouded mystery, proclaiming "I AM WHO I AM." To be committed to life is to experience this mysterium tremendum without the comforting beliefs and antiseptic platitudes of culture, religion or neurosis.

I would like to share my reflections on death with you. I hope my commitment to life can be heard, loud and clear. I hope you can see the siren call of uncommitment as well—"please let me go back to the safety of what I know." Most of all, I hope you feel understood or, at least, understanding.

DEATH

— I have been in analysis for many years.
— I have come to understand that my fear of death is a symptom of my fear of castration.
— I have come to understand that my fear of death is a symptom of my fear of total and irrevocable separation from Momma.
— I have come to understand that my fear of death is a derivative of my teenage panic over being sent to hell by an implacably just Roman Catholic god who despises nonconjugal sex.
— I have come to understand that all mortals fear death except those who are capable of denying it, which seems to be most people in most cultures as we all are surely immortal in one way or another.
— I understand all this, yet I understand almost nothing.
— This article is for the silent minority who stand mute while others answer the agonizing question of death with sure belief, certain knowledge, and clear credo.
— This article is for those who don't know what to say when a patient tells them he is dying of cancer.

— This article is for those who feel sudden, unmistakable panic when a patient casually informs them that she is having a CAT scan on an undiagnosed lump.

— This article is for therapists who are also parents who cannot bear the pain of looking at their child after reading another of those informative little articles about nuclear fallout.

— This article is for those therapists who, while listening to a patient casually conversing about reckless speeding, experience, not moral consternation or psychiatric concern, but total, unabashed human horror and bewilderment in the face of this other human being's capacity to talk about death glibly while death stands icily several feet away, waiting. For at that moment, I know that although I understand a great deal about defenses, and character structure, and denial of death embedded in our cultural myths and visions, I understand very little.

For we, who are described above, will read about heaven or the wisdom of surrendering to the VOID or reconciliation within aging or moving on or resurrection or quiet rest or reincarnation, and although we may explore each possibility with all our heart, spending days or years in the search, we end up always speechless. To those who stand before death in speechless terror, horror, awe, and wonderment without so much as a statement—never mind a whole credo worth of answers—I extend my greetings.

What I know can be held in a thimble, although I have looked long and often up to the sky and into the mirror. What I know is this: I love life so dearly that I cannot bear its loss; I know death so well that I treasure every minute of life. That's all I know. Life needs death and death needs life.

But if I could trade my beautiful thimble of knowing for immortality, I think I would jump at the chance. So far, no one has made me an offer.

So to those who stand with unshakable faith in life, but only speechless unknowing in the face of death; to those who know death, but have no credos and beliefs about death, I make this request—if death turns out to be a doorway to unknown adventure, let's look for each other. And if we need some comfort to overcome our initial terror and confusion, to leave behind our demons forever, let's ask and let's give. And then, in a wonderful grand finale, let's have a great laugh!

Comment

Any challenge to open my life more directly to the experience of the *mysterium tremendum* always excites me. The hero aspect of my psyche stirs from the comfortable resting place it usually shares with cowardice, laziness, fear, and routine. This article on the uncommitted patient, constellated my hero archetype. However, not to the point that I want to stand with the author, psychologically naked before the mystery of life. That mystery is both friendly and unfriendly, therefore a *tremendum*. Basically I want to be as close to the nuclear core of life as I can stand; but preferably in the robe of mystic rather than of psychotic.

The word commitment is difficult to define but some description of what the author means by it, would be helpful. I think free choice is an element of commitment and therefore I would hesitate to speak of patients and therapists as "deeply committed to their private illusions."

Unquestionably the word commitment is highly complex. On the one hand, it has an aspect of motion and becoming because it is a formal promise regarding the future. On the other hand, it contains a notion of fixity or permanence. It presumes that the similar ego identity and control over my total psyche that I now possess will continue in the future, so that I can deliver on the same promise. How can this happen in our world, presently seen as one of pervasive change? In addition, with our new understanding of ourselves as beings in process of becoming with others, people increasingly tend to shy away from commitments of any kind. They seem to fear the "fixity" aspect of commitment; that it will crush their process of becoming. This leads many to live provisionally, with both feet firmly planted in midair.

The positive aspect of commitment, as I view it, is that it gives me a certain rootedness and self-understanding. Through my choice in commitment I help my individuation and incarnation in the real world. I give up my Peter Pan fantasies for a flesh-and-blood existence with personal shadow. I dare to risk facing the real challenge of life's mystery.

There is a lot more to commitment than conscious choice. As a depth psychologist working from a Jungian perspective, I am convinced that only those conscious commitments which harmonize with the positive direction of our unconscious center of development, the Self, will be helpful to the person. This implies that the motivation for our deepest commitment remains partially unconscious.

I consider that clients who come to me have made a choice to pursue some healing. Whether they stay and promise to see the work through depends on many factors, conscious and unconscious. After first probing their conscious motivations, I use dream interpretation in the free mode of

Jungian understanding for the discernment of unconscious directions. When I can ascertain that the unconscious supports the client's conscious desire for analysis at this time, and in this manner under my guidance, it is easy to encourage the person's commitment. Naturally, this is not always the case. Such an approach, nevertheless, has many positive advantages for me and for the client. It confronts me with the basic mystery of each client's personality and the uniqueness of his or her development. It blocks impulses of mine to press for conscious commitment. Furthermore I do not so readily perceive lack of commitment as immediately signaling a defect in my skills or willful perversity on the part of the client.

The greatest advantage in considering commitment to be rooted in the unconscious psyche as well as in consciousness occurs through the process of dream analysis. Gradually, as I share with the client how dreams offer objective information compensating his or her conscious behavior, the client comes to value and commit himself or herself to the process. We do not focus on commitment, but I find that it grows quite naturally when the client understands that healing and wholeness do not come from the therapist but from his or her own guiding center.

Robert W. Baer, C.S.P., Ph.D.

The Hesitant Pilgrim

David S. Doane

"Unto whom much is given, of him shall much be required."

Luke 12:48

The word commitment means, according to Webster, "to send with" or "to connect" or "to entrust." The committed psychotherapy patient is committed to therapy, to growth. He is sent with his own growth, connected to and entrusted to growth.

To be committed to growth, the committed psychotherapy patient must be committed to self—not committed to ego, but committed to the authentic self. One engages in a process of allowing this self to come forth while openly noticing and listening to that real self. This is a goal-less process. This is a process of self-discovery. In this process, the individual is open to experimenting with and facilitating self, not manipulating or controlling that which we call self. In this process, the individual becomes a gateway for self. There is a sounding-through of self, which lies at the root meaning of person. This allowance of life is a demonstration of life living the person. The person committed to growth "lays down his life," gaining it by losing it. The committed psychotherapy patient is thus a disciple of self and its ways.

The uncommitted patient is not committed to growth, but rather is driven, trying to dictate life. Such living is an attempt to control life by attempting to achieve or prevent a particular outcome. With good intentions, the uncommitted individual may be trying to be an idealized person. However, this posture is a defensive one and is not conducive to letting the self grow. Such a person is holding on to being in a controlled way, and thus not gaining life.

With some who are uncommitted, there is the sense of their not having fully arrived at beginning psychotherapy. They hold themselves back from therapy and from the leap of commitment. The uncommitted patient may be in therapy for a considerable period of time. Yet the act of making appointments may simply be a flirtation with letting go before arriving fully and being committed to therapy.

David S. Doane, Ph.D., is a psychologist in full-time practice of psychotherapy. He is Director of the Crossroads Center in Toledo, Ohio.

Therapist: Do you think you'll ever get here?

Patient: What are you talking about? I'm here and have been coming for two months.

T: Well, your body's here, but I think you haven't fully arrived.

P: I'm here as much as I can be here.

T: I doubt that. You've hardly tested the water, but I'm hoping you'll jump in all the way.

When that patient finally jumps in, a commitment has taken place. Psychotherapy can now really begin. If the patient remains uncommitted, we don't make it. The following interaction happened with an uncommitted patient who began talking of terminating:

Patient: I don't think I'm going to come back.

Therapist: Come back? You haven't come yet.

P: You keep saying that.

T: Well, that's how it looks to me. How can you leave when you haven't yet arrived? I don't see this as an issue of quitting or leaving; I see it as you're not fully getting here as yet.

At times the uncommitted patient wants the experience of commitment without actually being committed. There then follows the issue of wanting the therapist to do the letting go. But this would be tantamount to a rape.

Patient: I don't want to cry.

Therapist: It looks to me like you're fighting hard not to cry.

P: What good will crying do?

T: You could find out.

P: (Continues to look painfully teary but says nothing.)

T: You're welcome to let go. I'm not willing to pull feelings out of you, but I am willing to be with you while you let them happen.

The uncommitted patient is equally frustrated and frustrating. Not letting go, the patient does not commit to a growth process. The psychotherapist notices the patient's uncommitment. It is up to the therapist to comment on this lack of true involvement. Nevertheless, the therapist has no known power to transform uncommitment to commitment. It's always the patient's life. And the patient has the right to remain less than committed. And the uncommitted patient may certainly gain from psychotherapy once the level of commitment is gained.

Comment

I continue to be astounded by the help that seems to materialize in the most mysterious ways just when needed. A few months ago the guest editor of this issue asked me to read and comment on several articles. In my fashion I parked them on my desk where they accumulated a significant covering of announcements, fliers, magazines.

It had been a devastating week. I had been wrestling with some significant personal issues for months, and in that week the effects of my preoccupation seemed to come crashing down on me. Several patients teed off on me, and more than a few announced plans to end therapy. By the end of the week I was ready to trade in my couch and began to think of other possible careers—computers, advertising, brain surgery (an interesting choice!)—but Friday was almost over, and I thought that I'd be able to regain my perspective over the weekend.

Andrew was a challenging patient: attractive, intelligent, charming; but I felt unable to really reach him. It was as if he were surrounded by a wall of thick glass bricks that transmitted glimmers of the light from behind it. The wall, however, was translucent not transparent, and I could neither feel nor truly see Andrew through it. He was a student in a particularly rigorous program that had some elements of unpredictability in it that he'd cancel appointments with short notice. He denied having any control over the situation, and he would not acknowledge that his resistance might ever be a factor.

For some weeks Andrew had been unable to reach anything that seemed significant in our sessions. The sessions themselves were disconnected and rambling; I had the feeling that Andrew was on the verge of something but I wasn't sure what it was or how to help him get to it. This particular Friday he walked into my office, crossed to his customary seat, sat, and after collecting himself announced that he'd decided to stop therapy "for a while." Even now I have trouble describing my reaction. I felt betrayed and devastated. "Hadn't I been working my tail off for him?" I thought, "What's going on?"

"What therapy?" I countered, "Just when therapy seems to be starting you disappear." Andrew looked hurt and began to deny my statement. "Your life seems dedicated to avoiding commitment."

The session proceeded apace, with me making such statements and Andrew fending them off. He left with his mind unchanged, and the crackle of hostility between us, but with his charm more or less intact. I sat without moving, feeling angry, drained, and impotent. After what seemed like a long time my eye drifted to the nascent paper skyscraper on my desk and I began to filter through it. Finding Dr. Doane's semi-forgotten paper seemed opportune, and I read it for the first time. I'm not sure what happened—perhaps it was the clarity of the described interactions or the assurance by another therapist that he, too, felt the power of the uncommitted—but I felt my spirits begin to lift. After a few more readings I felt my strength return and my disaster fantasies stop.

The next Monday Andrew walked into group and said to me, "After I left your office I began to feel real pissed off at you. I can't remember the last time I was so angry. In fact I spent the whole weekend yelling at people. Suddenly I realized that I felt more energetic than I'd felt in months. Maybe there's something to this therapy stuff after all."

Barry J. Wepman, Ph.D.

The "Terminating" Patient

Seymour E. Coopersmith

Some years ago, a woman in her early 30s began treatment with me, twice a week, in an effort to resolve serious interpersonal conflicts. After several sessions she aggressively confronted me with objections to continued treatment. Her first objection was to my fee. She claimed it was too high and, as a result, she could not afford the necessary two sessions a week. Secondly, she was disturbed by my appearance, claiming that I was not neat enough. This, she suggested, indicated that I had unresolved problems, and, as a consequence, would not be able to help her resolve her conflicts.

Attempts to resolve the issue of the "unfair" fee were met by her with demeaning, devaluating reactions to me although she continued treatment twice a week. During the year that she remained in treatment, she continually cited my "unfair" fee as a reason for termination. At other times she railed at me for not helping her enough and "not having it together enough" to help her. At these times she would ask me if I could recommend another therapist who would not have these "limitations." Consequently, she often threatened to terminate therapy. Her threats might be seen as a manifestation of paranoid anxieties which provoked a need in her to control me and the therapeutic process.

Patients with this particular defensive constellation, and perhaps others, might be identified as "terminating" patients. In order to understand such a "terminating" patient and her impact on the therapist and the therapeutic process, we need to consider, first, the concept of termination. Then we might consider how termination, when used as a threat, is a resistance to the development of a therapeutic alliance.

The experience of termination, in analytic therapy, usually has extensive emotional impact on both the patient and the therapist. Freud (1937, 1961), in "Analysis Terminable and Interminable," approached the concept of termination from the point of view of the goals and practical aspects of psychoanalysis. He suggested that an analysis was ended when the patient no longer suffered from symptoms and when the analyst judges "that so much repressed material has been made conscious, so

Seymour E. Coopersmith, Ed.D., is a psychoanalyst and supervisor in New York City. He is Past President of the National Psychological Association of Psychoanalysis (NPAP) and President-Elect of the Council of Psychoanalytic Psychotherapists.

63

much that was unintelligible has been explained, and so much internal re-sistance conquered, that there is no need to fear a repetition of the patho-logical processes concerned'' (p. 219). In his earlier writing, Freud in-dicated that this point has been reached when the transference neurosis has been resolved. From a more ambitious point of view, he indicated that an analysis is ended when no reasonable further change can be ex-pected. These conclusions imply relative degrees of treatment success: a patient, not too disturbed, who has been able to ''stay the course'' of treatment, and a focus on resolution of transference disturbance and dis-tortion. Freud's concern with termination focused on relatively neurotic patients, where termination was a bilateral and positive conclusion to treatment. This paper is concerned with more disturbed patients who have difficulty becoming involved or staying involved in treatment, and it will focus on the transference problems that interfere with treatment and sometimes lead to premature termination.

In recent years, with a shift to the investigation of countertransference (Searles, 1979; Epstein & Feiner, 1979), the impact of intense transfer-ence reactions on the therapist has been examined. Specifically, this paper will consider paranoid transference anxieties and the way they af-fect the therapist. These anxieties are often manifested by the patient in a constant threat, to the therapist, of termination. Consequently, this patient might be called a ''terminating'' patient—a patient who explicitly or im-plicitly, threatens the therapeutic process and the therapist with termina-tion.

THE NATURE OF TERMINATION

Behaviorally, termination is a psychoanalytically derived term which refers to the ending of the professionally conceived relationship between the patient and the therapist. It is a description of a process which implies ''completion'' or ''non-completion.'' It may be a consequence of bilater-al agreement between patient and therapist or it may be effected unilater-ally.

Many papers have been written about termination as a natural, bilateral completion of analysis which follows the ''working-through'' of un-conscious oedipal and pre-oedipal conflicts (Firestein, 1974; Freud, 1937; Glover, 1955; Lorand, 1946; Reich, 1950; Ticho, 1972). There has been less attention, however, to termination as a response to the pa-tient's pathological structures and to termination which is not bilaterally agreed upon by both patient and therapist. In most instances (excluding unavoidable reality interferences) these are terminations which are a con-sequence of transference and induced countertransference problems. These difficulties may lead to or be caused by the threat of termination itself. In other words, the threat of termination may have an effect on the therapist which may lead to the therapist acting in such a way as to provoke termination. For the therapist, the threat of termination may be experienced as the threat of abandonment. This experience may lead to a pressure on the therapeutic process which may further provoke a substantial deleterious influence on the transference-countertransference matrix.

THE TERMINATING PATIENT: A TRANSFERENCE CONDITION

A patient who constantly threatens termination—a terminating patient—is under the influence of intense anxieties which are provoked or heightened by the therapeutic interpersonal interaction. For example, a young woman came into treatment suggesting that all she wanted was someone who would give her specific guidelines and directives as to how she should lead her life. It became apparent, however, that she reacted to directions in a rebellious, resentful manner. She used this ploy as a way of controlling the treatment. When this was brought to her attention, she indicated her fear that she would become attached to me and that I would then reject her. During this period (about 6 months) she left therapy twice, to see other therapists, indicating, each time, that I was not practical enough and that she needed someone with a different approach to therapy. She was, in this early phase, a "terminating" patient with weak or primitive defenses against strong libidinal and aggressive drives. She was anxious that she would direct these intense, uncontrollable feelings toward me and that I would take advantage of her or ask her to leave treatment. Consequently, she always had one foot out the door.

Quite commonly, patients of this type, under the threat of paranoid anxieties, tend to seek release of these pressures through "acting out" or provoking the therapist to "act out." The therapist, however, is in a better position to deal with his or her own induced anxieties, when transference and countertransference manifestations are recognized and responded to by interpretation rather than acting out.

The terminating patient is the type of patient who threatens to leave therapy at an early stage of treatment, thus inhibiting the development of the therapeutic alliance. Initially, for example, the patient may question the therapist's credentials or qualities, may demand that therapy be restricted to a specific period of time, or may constantly seek to alter the financial or time-sequence contract.

In other instances, as treatment develops, and initial resistances are worked through, the developing intensity of the therapeutic involvement may lead to explicit or implicit threats of termination through acting-out behavior. These threats are often a consequence of weak or primitive defenses against sexual or aggressive drives directed toward significant internal objects and projected onto the therapist. The patient may then become so anxious that the therapist will strike out or abandon him or her that he or she threatens to leave the treatment.

These patients might be diagnosed as "borderline," as having weak or inadequate defenses against intensifying drives in the regressively developing transference. They have such weak ego boundaries that they easily develop a patient-therapist involvement which becomes too intense, too soon. In some cases, the patient falls in love with the therapist as a defense against fearful or angry feelings. In other cases, the patient identifies or merges with the therapist as a defensive maneuver. These defensive reactions may be particularly in evidence when transference resistance interpretations have been effective and internal self and object representations and relationship structures have been projected onto the therapist. Such a patient may have internalized an abandoning parent who always threatened (or in fact did abandon) the child for not being "good." As the parent controlled the child, so does the child attempt to control the therapist. The patient defends against the projected "persecutor" therapist, the envied therapist, or the desired but frustrating therapist. When this occurs, the patient feels impoverished, exposed, and vulnerable as a consequence of aggressive impulses which may be depressively directed inward or onto the therapist. The patient, feeling defenseless, considers termination, struggling for reintegration against primitive disintegrative processes.

THE REACTIONS OF THE THERAPIST
TO THE TERMINATING PATIENT

Most therapists are quite aware that they are not free of pathological dependencies, distorted self and object representations, and primitive as well as reasonable defense mechanisms. To some degree, every analysis will be influenced by the unresolved conflicts of the therapist. These conflicts may be a function of oedipal problems or they may be substantially influenced by more archaic pre-oedipal trauma. The latter centers on the separation matrix which may be influenced by depressive and paranoid tendencies. Consequently, it is important to keep in mind that the unconscious needs, wishes, or desires of the therapist may be activated by the patient. If, for example, the therapist seeks the patient's love, approval, or idealization, and this goal is seriously frustrated, the therapist may feel and act rejecting to the patient. The unacceptability of these angry feelings may invoke defense mechanisms (i.e., denial, splitting, reaction formation) or lead to acting out, which is in collusion with the defenses of the terminating patient.

If we can assume that any therapist could experience virtually any defensive reactions when threatened, externally or internally, then we might consider what defense might be brought to bear—and with what patient. The multiplicity of variables implies a complexity beyond the scope of this paper. It is, however, reasonable to assume that there is a paranoid potential in all therapists and that this potential might be activated by threatening, aggressive patients sensitive to the vulnerabilities of their therapist.

Finally, in this chain of events, if the therapist actively attempts to help, cure, or satisfy the patient; and the patient's devaluating or negative transference inhibits or prevents this, the therapist may begin to desire termination of the treatment. Searles (1979), in his paper on "Feelings of Guilt in the Psychoanalyst," suggests that: "In our guilt about not having made the right response, we fail to see the depth of the patient's ambivalence, the impossibility of there being any 'right' response that will somehow satisfy, simultaneously, both sides of his conflictual needs" (p. 33).

A meaningful therapeutic approach to this type of problematic situation lies in the interpretation of the "impossible" situation to the patient. Kernberg (1975) in his discussion on treatment of borderline patients with projective mechanisms, points out that "The direct consequences of the patient's hostile onslaught in the transference, his unrelenting efforts to push the therapist into a position in which he finally reacts with counter-aggression and the patient's sadistic efforts to control the therapist, can produce a paralyzing effect on the therapy" (p. 99). The patient's aggressive, controlling pressures have particular impact on the therapist when the patient accuses the therapist of insincerity, insensitivity, or inadequacy. The latter accusation is often implied—that is, the patient implies that the therapist is inadequate because of not fulfilling his or her "reasonable" needs. Guilt feelings (and resentment for these guilt feelings) in the therapist for not satisfying the demands or needs of the patient may lead the therapist to implicitly and explicitly reject the patient. In counter-response, the patient, sensing the condemning reacting of the therapist, begins to consider the alternative of termination or becomes a terminating patient. Thus, the sado-masochistic cycle is collusively enacted rather than interpreted. The missing link, in this situation, is a therapist (observing) ego which allows the therapist to understand and interpret the sado-masochistic bind between the patient and the therapist.

The terminating patient may represent, for the therapist, treatment failure, a symbolic representation of castration and object loss, a narcissistic wound. As a consequence, the therapist may act out feelings of aggression by accusing the patient of "running away from the treatment." Intersystemic and intrasystemic balances of ego and superego, in the therapist, are disrupted if there is an experience of disproportionate guilt or anxiety concerning a patient's projected termination. The therapist's experience is disproportionate to the extent that the therapist becomes overinvolved in the patient's termination agenda. Feelings of low self-regard may be induced in the therapist and manifested by exhibitionistic or grandiose acting out. Unconsciously, the therapist may be retaliating for the patient's rejecting or hostile transference. The following case vignette illustrates the operation of unconscious factors:

A patient told me about her prior therapist and how he had to impress her with his importance at a nearby hospital. This occurred when the patient was seeking a consultation for an evaluation of her treatment with him. But this was not the prime issue. The basic problem was that she was never able to get angry at him. He defended himself against her aggression by closing his eyes and leaning back in his chair. She was convinced he was asleep and when she asked him if he was asleep, he would open his eyes and say, "I think better with my eyes closed." She retaliated for his real or imagined withdrawal by calling him and engaging in long conversations over the weekend. He, perhaps because of his guilt feelings, was trapped by her sadistic manipulations. And when she complained that she wasn't feeling better or getting better, he suggested antidepressant medication. She mentioned termination several times, but he did not respond. At one point she came to see me for a consultation. I tried to help her understand the nature of the dynamics in her relationship with her therapist and suggested she try to work through the impasse. A year later she terminated her therapy with him.

In some instances, when termination is threatened, the therapist's understanding of the transference and resistance may be muted by depressive or paranoid reactions. In these situations, the therapist, who has a *mea culpa* response to the patient's implicit aggression, personifies a depressive defense; while the therapist who "accuses" the patient of using termination as a personal attack may actually be involved in a paranoid defensive reaction.

It is important for the therapist to be aware that the patient's transferences and resistances manifest self and object conflicts which are projected onto the therapist. The degree to which the therapist's unconscious "bad" self and object representations coincide with the patient's projections is the degree to which the therapist, defensively, is liable to believe or to respond collusively to the "stated" reason for termination.

Racker (1957), in "The Meanings and Uses of Countertransference," suggests that the analyst might identify, affectively, with the patient's central emotion (concordant identification); or, the analyst might identify with the internal objects of the patient, as projected onto the analyst (complementary identification). These countertransference identifications, and their affective components, are induced in the analyst. They constitute a powerful force which may be accepted, understood, and used in the service of the observing ego, or may sabotage the rational treatment efforts.

Such forces become extremely difficult for both patient and therapist when the threat of abandonment is intensified in the treatment process. What is significant for therapy continuity is the way the therapist experiences the pathological pressures of the terminating transference. The patient's transference may induce distortions of the therapist's understanding, behavior, and, in particular, of interpretations. Consequently, and conversely, the reactions induced in the therapist may so affect the therapist that they lead to a depressive projection onto the patient of the therapist's constellation of disruptive objects, structural interactions, and defense mechanisms.

There are, however, more productive responses to induced reactions. The therapist's response to induced reactions may be under the aegis of the observing ego and, consequently, be an important tool for transference understanding and conflict-resolving interpretations. Likewise, analysis of the patient's fantasies about the therapist's reactions to the idea of termination may be central to an interpretation of the patient's underlying transference anxieties. We proceed from the point of view that analysis involves an interaction of multiple forces between and within the personalities of both patient and therapist, under the aegis of the reasonably rational observing ego of the therapist. Then, the terminating transference becomes an understood and controlled aspect of treatment rather than a stultifying force which leads to premature termination.

THE TRANSFERENCE-COUNTERTRANSFERENCE "BIND"

When the terminating patient responds to the therapist as if he or she were a persecuting object (as well may be) and the therapist identifies with that object, a transference-countertransference "bind" occurs. The patient's paranoid anxiety has become objectified by the analyst's personification of the patient's internal sadistic imago. Thus, the therapist is both the object and subject of attack, abandonment, and even seduction. We can surmise that this depends on the degree to which the therapist has a pathological identification with the patient's pathological self and object representations.

The patient, on the other hand, experiences the therapist as an embodiment of the abandoning characteristics of projected internal objects. At the same time, the therapist is reacting with a complementary identification (Racker, 1957) in response to masochistic provocations. The totality is a paranoid-depressive structure (Klein, 1935/1975) in which the (superego) therapist persecutes the patient with (intellectualized) reproaches and threatens abandonment (i.e., referral to another therapist). Summarily, the patient's aggression creates anxiety which leads to counteraggression by the therapist and, perhaps, a preemptive end to the therapeutic process. The patient, fearing he or she will be a helpless victim of the therapist's sadism, withdraws and rejects the therapist by threatening termination. The merger of the patient's persecutory imagos with those of the therapist makes for a sadomasochistic cycle as both therapist and patient identify with an aggressive imago. This internal process may lead to defensive behavioral reactions of boredom, sleepiness, collusive emotional withdrawal, or other varieties of acting out in both patient and therapist. The ultimate effect of this transpiration is that the patient is unable to be dependent on a persecutory object, and, consequently, rejects the therapist's unsavory (in this instance) interpretations—while the therapist, in response, feels muted and ineffective.

RESOLUTION OF THE TRANSFERENCE-COUNTERTRANSFERENCE BIND WITH THE TERMINATING PATIENT

Given the power of the unconscious forces at work in both patient and therapist, resolution of this problem is often difficult and sometimes impossible. The observing capacity of the well-integrated ego of the therapist, however, provides an opportunity for the interruption or reversal of resistive countertransference involvement and the uncovering or reestablishment of a constructive treatment process. The reduction of the transference-countertransference bind leads itself to a consideration of the following: (1) Self-analysis in the transference-countertransference interaction; (2) genetic self-analysis (i.e., who or what does the patient represent in the therapist's psychic history; and (3) the use of the patient's "material": (i.e., images, perceptions, and fantasies of the therapist) as a guide to understanding the anxieties of the patient (Langs, 1983).

In addition to self-awareness of his or her own psychic makeup, the therapist needs to probe his or her feelings and examine any defensive reactions to the terminating transference. The therapist needs to be particularly on guard against the development of sadomasochistic feelings and reactions. The therapist who is masochistically passive (in the face of the terminating transference) is neglecting active interpretations of the transference, preoedipal conflict, and sadistic or paranoid defenses against these interpretations.

Active and empathically appropriate interpretations can, however, break the pattern. Such responses are in clear contrast to the machinations of the frustrated therapist who encourages or solicits angry outbursts in the hope that this will free the patient from repressed or suppressed aggression. The success of the interpretations will depend primarily on the therapeutic alliance and the degree to which the analyst's interpretations are nonpersecutory. The complications involved in the resolution of the transference-countertransference bind are influenced substantially by the nature and strength of the patient's ego boundaries and receptivity to dilemma-resolving interpretations. The therapist's theoretical comprehension of the patient-therapist structure can liberate positive feelings and empathic responses to the patient. Awareness of countertransference anxieties are essential if the therapist is to provide dilemma-resolving interpretations which reduce anxiety and prevent termination.

A case in point involves a single male in his late 20s who was referred by a former patient for psychotherapy. When he called for an appointment he explained that he was a recent veteran of the Vietnam war and had to talk to someone who was familiar with the atrocities that had taken place during the war. My first response was to take him at (content) face value and to seek out a referral to a therapist with extensive experience with veterans. Because it was midsummer and there were few therapists with the requested background available, it was difficult to make an appropriate referral. So I asked the prospective patient if he wanted to see me, even though I had no prior experience with Vietnam atrocities. He readily agreed and we arranged the first appointment. After several sessions it became apparent that Vietnam atrocities were a smoke screen, so to speak, for his anxieties about atrocities in his mind that he feared might emerge in the therapeutic process.

During the first few months of therapy, development of an alliance was difficult because of his devaluation of me and the treatment process. He wasn't sure therapy would or could provide the solution to his problems. "I should," he said, "handle this by myself." But he stayed in treatment, twice a week, even though he came to sessions with headaches. After about 6 months, he said, "This has gone far enough—nothing is happening—I'd better stop coming in." This minor crisis was handled empathically (i.e., "This whole process must be difficult—particularly where you get concerned about one or both of us getting mad") as well as interpretively. Although he could not acknowledge his angry feelings, he was satisfied with the idea that I knew what was going on and that there would be no loss of control on either of our parts.

My reactions during this early phase fluctuated considerably, particularly when he devaluated me, or the therapeutic process. My feelings of frustration and resentment were counterbalanced by my awareness of his fragility and vulnerability. He was hostile toward me when he needed to defend himself against anticipated abuse. When I pointed this out to him, he told me how his father had beaten him as a child and then died suddenly of a heart attack when my patient was 16 years old. At other times, he was quite bitter toward me, complaining that things were getting worse rather than better and that it might be better if he stopped coming to see me. Several times I became quite discouraged and considered recommending that he should see a different therapist. But when I was able to understand the induced nature of my reactions, I suggested that he would like me to give up because he was frightened of trusting me, afraid that I would abuse him (by raising his fee) or that I would abandon him (i.e., ask him to leave if he lost his job and couldn't afford to pay for therapy). Eventually he acknowledged these anxieties as well as his anger toward me. When this happened, his threat to terminate emerged less frequently, consistent with his diminished accusations. Concurrently, my anger and anxiety abated as my empathic response to his fragility and neediness increased. The threat to terminate emerged infrequently after the first 4 years of treatment.

This case illustrates how the continuity of treatment of a paranoid borderline patient can be disrupted by paranoid anxiety, manifested by the threat to terminate treatment. Anxieties induced by the patient almost caused the therapist to terminate the treatment. Interpretations of the transference-countertransference struggle and an empathic sense of the patient's vulnerability helped reduce anxieties and tensions until the terminating structure was reduced and the therapeutic alliance enhanced.

SUMMARY

The effect of aggressive drives on object relations is a significant aspect of the impact of patient transference and therapist countertransference reactions on each other. This issue is often most intense early in the treatment process when paranoid anxieties evoke varying degrees of aggression and depression in both patient and therapist. These reactions are often manifested defensively with the threat of termination or actual termination.

This paper explores the crisis which develops when the two parties to the treatment situation are both anxious and defensively responsive to each other's internalized processes. The reactions of the patient to unconscious paranoid anxieties can lead to threats of termination. The reactions of the therapist to transferential forces, particularly those involving aggressive drives, can be of an unconscious acting-out nature, or can be consciously controlled and, consequently, be an effective interpretive aspect of treatment. The essential problem for the therapist involves the way he or she responds to his or her own aggression, whether it has its origins in countertransference or is induced by the patient. Several brief clinical examples are provided to illustrate how paranoid anxieties can affect both patient and therapist, such that the patient becomes a terminating patient and the therapist is subject to his or her own anxious reactions, leading to nonconstructive interpretations of a paranoid nature. An alternative to acting out, an interpretive approach, provides an opportunity to break through the transference-countertransference bind and reduce the anxieties and pressures of the terminating patient.

REFERENCES

Epstein, L., & Feiner, A. H. (1979). *Countertransference.* New York: Jason Aronson.

Firestein, S. (1974). Termination of psychoanalysis of adults: A review of literature. *Journal of the American Psychoanalytic Association, 22* (4), 873-893.

Freud, S. (1961). Analysis terminable and interminable. In J. Strachey (Ed. & Trans.), *The standard edition of the complete psychological works of Sigmund Freud* (Vol. 23, pp. 209-254). London: Hogarth Press. (Original work published 1923).

Giovacchini, P. (1973). Countertransference problems. *International Journal of Psychotherapy, 1,* 112-127.

Giovacchini, P. (1979). *Treatment of primitive mental states.* New York: Jason Aronson.

Glover, E. (1955). Termination. In *Techniques of Psychoanalysis* (pp. 134-164). New York: International Universities Press.

Goldberg, A. (1975). Narcissism and the readiness for psychotherapy termination. *Archives of General Psychiatry, 32* (6), 695-699.

Gottesfeld, M. L. (1980). When the therapist wants to terminate: From pessimism to the grotesque. *VOICES: The Art and Science of Psychotherapy, 16* (2), 14-15.

Kernberg, O. (1975). *Borderline conditions and pathological narcissism.* New York: Jason Aronson.

Kernberg, O. (1980). *Internal world and external reality.* New York: Jason Aronson.

Klein, M. (1975). A contribution to the psychogenesis of manic-depressive states. In *Love, guilt, and reparation.* New York: Delacorte Press/Seymour Lawrence. (Originally published 1935).

Lorand, S. (1946). Termination. In *Techniques of psychoanalytic therapy* (pp. 223-232). New York: International Universities Press.

Racker, H. (1957). The meanings and uses of countertransference. *Psychoanalytic Quarterly, 26,* 303-357.

Racker, H. (1963). *Transference and countertransference.* New York: International Universities Press.

Reich, A. (1950). On the termination of analysis. In *Psychoanalytic Contributions* (pp. 121-135). New York: International Universities Press.

Searles, H. (1979). *Countertransference and related subjects: Selected papers.* New York: International Universities Press.

Ticho, E. (1972). Termination of psychoanalysis, treatment goals, life goals. *Psychoanalytic Quarterly, 41,* 315-333.

The Uncommitted Client in a Short-Term Treatment Setting

Kathryn Welds

Discussions of the practical aspects of a psychotherapy private practice frequently note that Freud was among the first psychiatrists to assert that client responsibility for the cost of therapy enhances client motivation for treatment and "cure." Delivery of mental health services has changed dramatically since Freud's time and two recent developments may impede clients' commitment to treatment by removing them from direct responsibility for payment, and thus, for "working" in treatment. Greater reliance upon health-maintenance organizations which provide a variety of services for a single fee, as well as third-party reimbursement for psychotherapy hallmark this change. Related developments stress the value of shorter-term therapies and behaviorally based treatments as cost-cutting measures which purportedly enhance client motivation.

One example of this type of treatment setting is a community college psychological service. While working as a psychologist in one such center which specialized in crisis intervention and short-term treatment offered to students for the nominal, one-time health fee, I met and treated so many uncommitted clients that I began to wonder about the validity of the assertion of enhanced motivation. In addition, three questions emerged in thinking about treatment planning:

1. Is it possible to forecast "lack of commitment" from the initial interview?
2. What should the therapist use as indicators of countertransference reactions to uncommitted clients?
3. What strategies might be used to mobilize treatment with uncommitted clients?

Kathryn Welds, Ph.D., is a psychologist and continuing-education specialist who coordinates courses on personal development and women's studies for mental health professionals and lay audiences at the University of California at Los Angeles Extension.

Thoughts concerning these questions come from both personal successes and errors in dealing with a difficult and volatile population, as well as from the observed case management by interns assigned for supervision from a psychoanalytically oriented graduate program. The case presented here is far from successful, but is offered because it illustrates both possible points of intervention as well as some of the pitfalls in dealing with uncommitted clients.

In considering the question of clinical prediction of commitment to treatment, Enright (1975) suggests that

> "Motivation for psychotherapy" is a central determinant of the degree of movement of success in the process of therapy. . .(and) many failures are attributed to "low motivation". . . . (Though) motivation is complex, one facet, the expressed willingness to be there, on the part of the patient, can be isolated and studied quite easily. (p. 1)

Though this expressed willingness to be physically present is no guarantee of a positive outcome, Enright maintains that its absence "is a frequent and powerful drag on the therapeutic process" (p. 10).

An additional factor important in the better prediction of commitment to treatment centers on *how* a client arrived at treatment, that is, at whose suggestion or demand. In institutional settings like the college, referrals from third parties, such as disgruntled professors, parents, or parole officers most often produce unwilling and embittered clients. Given such an unfavorable setting for treatment, one wonders whether even skillful interventions can engender commitment. A complex case of a mother and daughter enrolled in the licensed vocational nursing program may offer more questions than answers about this problem.

Carmen, a 46-year-old Puerto Rican mother of three adolescent daughters, was enrolled in the Licensed Vocational Nurse program while she continued her successful career as a real-estate salesperson. She was discovered crying in a utility closet by her nursing instructor, and she was referred for individual treatment. She expressed her distress about class dissension and conflict propagated by several difficult students. In addition, she complained of depression and years of physical and emotional abuse by her husband, who had carried on numerous extramarital affairs. She was seen for 24 sessions by a psychoanalytically oriented intern who noted similarities in their life situations and expressed genuine liking for Carmen.

During the first session, Carmen stated that because of financial considerations, she "couldn't" leave her husband until she completed the nursing program. In addition, she said that she feared being single and "knew" that she wouldn't attract another husband. After the intern stressed the importance of severing an abusive marriage, Carmen "was astonished" when she failed her final examinations in the nursing program and was terminated.

She failed to attend the next four sessions and when she returned she revealed a "horrible secret." She said that she had been having an affair with a married man for 9 years and that he wanted to marry her. She was unable to explain why she wouldn't dissolve her marriage for this man since this seemed the answer to her concern about finding another man. She again failed to attend the next two sessions, which came before the intern's extended vacation, going to see her fiancé in a distant city. Toward the end of the intern's time at the center, Carmen became depressed and angry, although the therapist's final note stated that Carmen's functioning had improved but that "the leave-taking experience recapitulates the client's early reaction to her father's death."

The center had no further contact with Carmen, but after 6 months, her 20-year-old daughter, Sonya, was referred by the same nursing instructor, who noted her poor performance in the clinical portion of the nursing program. Sonya stated her resentment at the referral but denied irritation with her mother, who insisted that she enroll in nursing rather than in her preferred career choices—cosmetology or travel-agency management.

Sonya admitted that she felt like a "dumping ground" for her mother's anger toward her father and she saw that Carmen might be trying to fulfill her own thwarted career aspirations through Sonya. She said that she complied with her mother because "I owe so much to my mother—she had me when she was only 16." Though she stated rage at nursing professors who "try to boss me around," "treat me like a child," and "call me immature," she refused to evoke her mother's anger, resentment, and rage by exerting any type of autonomy. She refused further contact with the office and the therapist felt powerless to intervene in this vocational "folie à deux." Family treatment was recommended and refused.

A month later, Sonya was again referred to the center for her continuing poor performance in clinical nursing. She was seen by an experienced male therapist who prescribed behavioral measures to improve performance, but he did not consider the more fundamental question of whether she was interested in or well suited to the nursing program. She failed to attend her subsequent appointment during which she was supposed to report upon her homework.

This case illustrated the difficulties of *ad hoc* referrals in large treatment settings where clients may be assigned to various therapists with differing orientations. This structural difficulty can only underscore a client's flagging interest in therapy, and it serves to absolve the therapist of responsibility for therapeutic failures by keeping the client at a distance.

In contrast, the minor success of engaging Carmen in treatment, even sporadically, points to the importance of a positive affective connection between therapist and client. If the intern had continued to work at the center, one might speculate that Carmen could have become more fully engaged in a longer term treatment and could have made some significant gains in clarifying her continued involvement in both an unsatisfying marital relationship as well as in a clandestine affair, her controlling relationship with her daughters, and her inability to release them to develop their own independent competence in vocational and interpersonal spheres. The case offers a contrast between the intern's ability to connect with Carmen, and the complete failure of two experienced therapists to attract Sonya and retain her as a client even when she was rather forcefully coerced into the consultation situation.

One explanation of this discrepancy is offered by colleagues who work in this type of setting. Success in engaging uncommitted clients is heavily dependent not only upon the therapist transmitting positive regard for the client, but also on willingness to "pitch the benefits of treatment." These colleagues attribute therapeutic success to an active, "sales-oriented" approach in working with uncommitted clients.

For those who find this line of thinking incompatible with personal style, Enright (n.d.) again offers an alternative view of the concept of therapeutic commitment and appropriate treatment strategies:

> . . . the notion of "resistance" is absurd . . . (I have decided) to look for other, more effective ways of describing/understanding the phenomenon usually classified as "resistance"—as stubbornness or stupidity on the part of the client—I will look on as lack of understanding or clarity on the part of the therapist, possibly resulting from gaps or rigidities in her or his frame of reference. I will take the position that if the client seems to "resist" it simply means that she/he knows something we don't, and our job is to find out as rapidly as possible what it might be.

Enright, then, is suggesting that the active therapist is more an investigator than a salesperson of mental health benefits, and this approach offers some advantages over taking full responsibility for even hoping to control therapeutic gains of "successes." This can lead to an egocentric connection to the client's progress in which the client and therapist come dangerously close to developing an umbilical connection and reliance upon the other for guidance and definition of self-worth.

Langs (1979) defined this situation as countertransference, "all inappropriate and pathological responses of the therapist to . . . (the) patient. These restrictions are founded on pathological unconscious fantasies, memories, introjects, and interactional mechanisms" (p. 538). These pathological reactions can center on the therapist's own need to be an effective, competent, well-liked savior of the uncommitted client who is caught in the conundrum outlined by Singer and Miller (1983):

1. I'm an adult so I should be able to manage my life.
2. I can't so I'm seeking help.
3. If I permit you to help, I'm confirming my incompetence to manage my life.
4. The only way to demonstrate my competence is to resist change.

When working with such clients, it may be difficult for the therapist to avoid being caught in an oppositional web, and he or she may resort to three compensatory strategies outlined by Kohut (1982): withdrawal, boredom, and compulsive activity. He suggests that these responses are evoked if the client begins to develop a merging/twinship transference, also called a mirror transference. This can evoke alarm in the therapist, and these countertransference maneuvers are a defensive attempt to preserve a sense of personal integrity and autonomy from the client's psychic intrusions. Such responses fail to make the therapeutic contact narcissistically gratifying to the client, and this reinforces resistance and lack of commitment (Singer & Miller, 1983).

In recognizing this process, Davanloo (1978) comments that the therapist and client in a short-term framework are vulnerable to forming a misalliance directed toward some form of shared defensiveness rather than toward some type of insight. Similarly, Searles (1979) discusses the possible iatrogenic (therapist induced) difficulties inherent in the therapist-client relationship when he defines "*Countertransference induction* or *countertransference grafting* . . . (as the well-known danger) of the analyst's 'inducing' or 'grafting' his own neurosis upon the patient'' (p. 125). This process was noted in many examples from the center as in Hoyt and Farrell's (1983) courageous discussion of a dramatic episode in a short-term contact with a man experiencing post-traumatic stress syndrome following his wife's suicide.

To intervene in the sometimes imperceptible process of countertransference, Langs (1979) offers the following recommendation: "Remember: Therapist before patient. Once you have ferreted out your contributions to such behavior, you would then be in a position to identify those that stem from the patient's own pathology'' (p. 371). Similarly, Enright (1975) argues that the therapist must avoid the type of defensive manipulation often seen among therapists and described by Gillis (1974). He goes so far as to advocate the therapist's complete neutrality, in even allowing the client to stay for only as much of the session as deemed helpful, paying for that portion only. He states that this avoids collusion with clients who come to sessions but remain intractable and whose passive aggression is manifested by their lack of commitment to therapy. This type of innovative therapeutic structure may go beyond quelling and managing toxic countertransference reactions and it may be the type of unexpected intervention that will enage and mobilize uncommitted clients.

Perhaps an important message emerges for clinicians who have been treating more affluent, verbal, intellectually oriented clients for longer periods of time. With changing structures of health-care delivery and reimbursement, the problem of the uncommitted client may touch even the most selective of therapists. Recognizing a major predictor of commitment to treatment—stated willingness to participate—may be just as important as recognizing the untherapeutic countertransference reactions which may arise from the frustrations in treating uncommitted clients. Constant awareness of dangerous countertransference dynamics such as withdrawal, boredom, and compulsive activity, shares equal importance with openness to considering innovative therapeutic structures to engage the uncommitted client.

REFERENCES

Davanloo, H. (Ed.). (1978). *Basic principles and techniques in short term dynamic psychotherapy.* New York: Spectrum.

Enright, J. (1975). One step forward: Situational techniques for altering motivation for therapy. *Psychotherapy: Theory, Research & Practice, 14*(4), 344-347.

Enright, J. (n.d.). Therapy without resistance. Unpublished paper. Richmond, CA: ARC Associates.

Gillis, J. S. (1974, December). The therapist as manipulator. *Psychology Today,* pp. 91-95.

Hoyt, M. F., & Farrell, D. (1982, February). Countertransference difficulties in a time-limited psychotherapy. Paper presented at California State Psychological Association, San Francisco, CA.

Kohut, H. (1982). *The analysis of the self.* New York: International Universities Press.

Langs, R. (1979). *The therapeutic environment.* New York: Jason Aronson.

Singer, M. T., & Miller, J. S. (1983, May). Diagnosis and psychotherapy of personality disorders. Seminar presented at University of California, Los Angeles Extension.

Norms, Commitment, and Psychotherapy With the Involuntarily Hospitalized Psychiatric Patient

Patricia J. Parsons

Commitment, or the state of being emotionally impelled to a particular course, is an important issue in psychotherapy for both the therapist and the patient. The therapist must be committed to helping the patient and the patient must be committed to "working" in therapy and to change of some sort. Lack of commitment can be a difficult problem with the typical patient seen in private practice, in mental health clinics, and other similar settings. Yet there is a clientele whose "lack of commitment" can be an even more problematical issue—the involuntary psychiatric patient.

THE UNCOMMITTED INVOLUNTARY PSYCHIATRIC PATIENT

In addition to the above-mentioned, commitment also refers to consignment to a mental institution. Individuals are committed to a psychiatric hospital in the United States for either one of two purposes. The first is protection of society or even of the individual because of his or her dangerousness. The second is treatment and care, determined by a psychiatrist to be in the client's best interest (*parens patriae* model). This commitment is most frequently involuntary—not under the client's own volition. Individuals committed to state psychiatric hospitals are a population who have traditionally "slipped through the cracks" or filtered through private practitioners, private psychiatric hospitals, general hospitals, community mental-health centers, county hospitals, and so forth to finally end up in a state psychiatric facility. These individuals have not been successfully treated or maintained in the community. They are, for the most part, *the most severely problematic patients* in need of treatment. Although described as a "captive audience" for psychotherapists, most psychiatric patients are not committed to their own treatment and thus to change. Such individuals frequently deny a need for treatment, adopt a

Patricia J. Parsons, Ph.D., is Director of Psychology, Greystone Park Psychiatric Hospital, Morris Plains, NJ, and a private practitioner.

passive life-style looking forward only to the next cigarette, or assault other individuals, and so forth. The wards of psychiatric hospitals are filled with such individuals, in need of treatment yet uncommitted to it. They might be described as the ''uncommitted committed.'' The following is a typical example of such a patient.

B.Z.: An Involuntarily Hospitalized Psychiatric Patient

B.Z. is a 23-year-old white male who was committed to a state psychiatric hospital for the second time. Prior to this more recent admission he was living at home with his parents. He became verbally abusive and physically assaultive—hitting his mother and breaking one of her ribs. His parents were unable to control him and so they returned him to the hospital. With the exception of an 18-month hiatus in the community, B.Z. has been in institutions almost continuously since age 17, when he was first hospitalized in a general hospital for an acute psychotic episode.

B.Z. is a very tall (6'2"), lanky young man. His clothing and hair are disheveled and his hygiene is very poor. He is a seclusive individual who tends to sit alone in a corner, giggling and talking to himself as if responding to auditory hallucinations. He is unable to carry on a conversation for more than a minute or so—frequently yelling out irrelevant comments. The Wechsler Adult Intelligence Scale revealed a Full Scale I.Q. of 80.

The biggest treatment problem is B.Z.'s unmanageability. The patient yells loudly and threatens other patients and staff. He has a lengthy history of assault and has attacked his mother, other patients, and staff (especially females) to such an extent that he has been confined for periods of time in the state facility for the criminally insane. A variety of medication has been tried on B.Z. with no notable results. His large size and history of assaultive behavior have made staff leery of him and with good reason. Several community programs terminated their involvement with him because of his outbursts and their (realistic) fear of injury.

This patient and others like him are often singularly uninterested in their own treatment or in anything else. Even families acknowledge and bemoan the lack of motivation of family members who are psychiatric patients to ''get better.'' Such patients remain in the institution for long periods and will not improve or even maintain their current level of functioning over time if dismissed as candidates for treatment.

THE UNCOMMITTED THERAPIST

Lack of commitment by an involuntarily hospitalized patient is doubly problematic if the therapist is also not committed to treating such patients. Theoretically all patients in state psychiatric hospitals have potential therapists because professional staff (e.g., psychologists, social workers, etc.) are assigned to wards of patients. However, high staff-to-patient ratios (a ratio of one professional staff member for 50 patients is not unusual) complicate the issue. In such a situation the typical psychotherapist selects six to eight patients from among the ward as candidates for long-term, dynamically oriented psychotherapy. The "best" patients receive the personal attention of the therapists on a bi-weekly basis. Individuals like B.Z. are rarely selected for psychotherapy. The expression, lack of commitment, can also be applied to the potential therapist who often lacks the commitment to treat many psychiatric patients. Few therapists want to treat a patient who will not talk, who is only concerned with the next cigarette, or who has a history of assaultive behavior and shakes his fist in the therapist's face.

NORMS AND COMMITMENT

Before commitment to something new can occur it is necessary to determine to what the group or individual is, at this point in time, already committed. If this is determined to be undesirable, then there can be a re-commitment of energies to something else. Toward this end norms must be examined. The norms or expected behaviors of individuals within a group are major factors in determining the behavior of an individual member. Sometimes these norms are spoken messages transmitted from the group to the individual and thus the individual can articulate the norm. Frequently these norms are unspoken messages, thus denying the individual involved the opportunity to verbalize the norm, to examine it, and to freely choose patterns of behavior for himself or herself. Unless norms can be articulated and examined, and a commitment made to adopt new, freely chosen norms then change will not occur (Allen & Kraft, 1980;1982).

NORMS AND PSYCHOTHERAPISTS

In the clinical area, as in other areas of life, norms or expected behaviors exist. Psychotherapists are influenced by the norms of their peer groups, be they psychiatrists, psychologists, social workers, or nurses. Norms about what is done in psychotherapy, about what form of therapy to employ, and about who should receive psychotherapy are powerful determinants of psychotherapists' behavior, yet these norms about clinical treatment are rarely articulated and examined. (One notable examination of clinical values is by Halleck, 1981. Values, however, are different from norms. Values are abstract principles felt to be intrinsically valuable to the individual. Norms are ways of behaving, and values may or may not be carried out in behaviors. Norms are also accompanied by social sanctions.) It is vital to begin to identify some of these norms and to obtain individual and group commitment to make changes if this is desired.

The reason for the dismissal of many psychiatric patients as psychotherapy candidates can be understood by looking at the training and background of psychotherapists and by making some guesses as to the norms underlying such behavior. Most psychotherapists were trained to treat—usually by psychoanalytically oriented, individual psychotherapy—a population quite different from psychiatric patients who will not talk and participate in intensive, in-depth, insight-oriented therapy. Most psychotherapists, in the course of their training, learn to value personal growth in patients and feel gratified by change in their patients. In contrast, psychiatric patients are often singularly unrewarding and highly problematic to the therapist. Some patients, who both seek and reject help, if they do begin to participate in therapy, do not keep appointments, drop in at unusual times, find the therapist throughout the hospital at odd moments during the day, and frequently do not follow through with even the most basic tasks. If permitted, these patients will drain staff time, energy, and resources. Such patients deny the therapist the opportunity to facilitate personal growth and improvement—something which is very rewarding to psychotherapists. And, psychiatric patients are rarely "cured." They often do not see their role in their problems. In private practice most therapists are especially gratified and feel competent when they can see evidence of patient change. With the involuntarily hospitalized psychiatric patient the therapist is most likely to feel anger, annoyance, frustration, and helplessness as a result of interactions with patients. Frequently psychotherapists, either before attempting therapy if they are familiar with psychiatric patients and facilities or after some futile experience with such patients if they are new to the clientele and the situation, dismiss the patient saying, "unmotivated people can't be helped." It is then tempting to blame the therapist for a lack of commitment in the same way that the therapist blames the patient for a lack of commitment. This approach, singularly unproductive, neglects the role of group norms or expectations determining the behavior of the individual. Dismissal of patients as psychotherapy candidates saying they are "uncommitted" or "unmotivated" is an accepted behavior among many psychotherapists—a professional norm. Moreover, Stein and Test (1982) believe such a comment is evidence of poor clinical judgment, and lack of motivation or commitment is a part of the patient's illness.

The norms of the graduate school, the professional group, and co-workers on the job have profound effects on the behavior of the individual psychotherapist. If the unspoken norm is that most psychiatric patients are not "treatable" then therapists are not truly engaged in treating them. It is interesting to note the effect of group norms on psychiatric residents' treatment of psychotic patients (Halleck, 1982). Psychiatric residents were told that their performance evaluation would be based on their ability to keep their psychotic patients out of a psychiatric hospital and involved in out-patient therapy. When the articulated norms of a group of psychiatric residents were that psychotic patients belonged in individual therapy and that it was the responsibility of the resident to keep the patient in therapy, such patients remained in and benefited from therapy. Compliance with treatment appointments by patients was outstanding and rehospitalization was rare. This suggests the efficacy of results with difficult patients with a change in the norms to which individual psychotherapists adhere. The culture of most therapists makes working with psychiatric patients low in status, reinforces the use of individual, in-depth, insight-oriented therapy and encourages a focus on personal growth despite increasing evidence that this approach neglects the role of social factors in the genesis and maintenance of maladaptive behaviors (e.g., Falloon, Boyd, McGill, Razani, Moss, & Guilderman, 1982). Unfortunately, there has been no formal examination of the norms of professional groups of individuals providing psychotherapy to psychiatric patients. Again, such norms need to be articulated so that they can be examined by professionals who provide psychotherapy services so that they can decide whether they want to espouse norms which, in a state psychiatric setting, result in clinical-service delivery to a very few.

THE COMMITTED FAMILY

If neither the patient nor the average psychotherapist is committed to the patient's treatment, it is indeed fortunate that the family is frequently strongly committed to helping the patient. It has been estimated that 50-66% of patients are discharged to return home to their families. Moreover, many families maintain contact with and are willing to assist family members who are psychiatric patients over a long period of time (Minkoff, 1979). Evidence also indicates that they are aware of and can articulate the lack of motivation in their hospitalized family member (e.g., Hatfield, 1979).

It is time to effectively utilize this family commitment to help the psychiatric patient. Although Hatfield (1979) wrote the following statement about chronic schizophrenic patients, this author has found her comments to be true for almost all psychiatric patients. Hatfield writes:

A team approach involving families and professionals is needed for the care and rehabilitation of chronic schizophrenics. Families often have deep commitment and first-hand knowledge, information about services and supports, and objectivity and skill. New modalities of treatment and rehabilitation that spell out a collaborative approach are now in order. A different kind of professional and a different kind of training are needed. (p. 340)

She further comments:

Given their unshakable commitment and the basic understanding of the patient they have gained through total immersion, these families are an invaluable resource in treatment and rehabilitation. (p. 340)

Fortunately, there is a growing tendency to utilize the commitment and enlist the involvement of the family in the care of the patient (e.g., Goldstein, 1981). A psychotherapist who is actively engaged in treating psychiatric patients might elect to use this family commitment in a constructive way *after* helping the family examine current norms and behaviors. Families, like professional groups, have norms. Rules, procedures, and so forth, are verbalized (e.g., speaking rudely to a family member is not permitted) and unverbalized (e.g., B.Z. is mentally ill and normal conversation cannot be expected but hitting people *is* expected, men in the family need not talk, mother is responsible for B.Z.). The task of the psychotherapist is to help the family uncover and articulate these norms so that the family can question them and redirect their commitment to the patient in a direction that will help the patient change. In B.Z.'s family there are parallels between the parents' style of withdrawing, not talking, and avoiding areas of conflict or problems and B.Z.'s style of not talking but becoming violent and assaultive when something is bothering him. When B.Z.'s family was helped to articulate their belief (not uncommon) that since he is mentally ill they should not expect decent conversation from him and that hitting *is* acceptable they were able to make the decision that this is not what they want for a family norm. Helping the family to verbalize the norm that men (including B.Z., his father, his brothers) are not expected to talk about things that bother them is helping them evaluate whether they want to accept this norm or commit themselves to changing it. Stating and discussing the norm that all the responsibility for B.Z.'s care rests with his mother has helped her to allow and to encourage her husband to participate more in B.Z.'s care and to decrease her overinvolvement. B.Z. is more responsive under his father's guidance and male modeling. The family is learning to set appropriate limits with B.Z., to openly discuss their feelings and provide consequences for his assaults on others, to reinforce appropriate behaviors, and to cope more appropriately with B.Z.'s illness (via increased involvement by his father and decreased involvement by his mother). Thus, the psychotherapists' commitment to providing therapy to an involuntarily hospitalized patient with the assistance of a family who is highly committed to helping the patient is beginning to ''pay off'' for the patient. Treatment will continue, and perhaps for a long period of time, but this is feasible because the mode of treatment is a multiple-family group with several other families. An added advantage of having a number of families in the group is that B.Z.'s family is now being exposed to group family norms quite different from their own.

SUMMARY

One definition of commitment is the state of being emotionally impelled to a particular course. Commitment to change is viewed as an important factor in psychotherapy. Prior to obtaining commitment to change it is necessary to determine the group-defined norms or expected behaviors of individuals, to articulate them, and to question their usefulness for the individual's needs and goals. This suggests that an examination of the lack of commitment by a psychotherapist to provide therapy for a psychiatric patient, and the lack of commitment by the patient to therapy necessitates an evaluation of norms of the therapist's professional group and the patient's family. After norms are examined, hopefully a freely made choice of the psychotherapist and the family to recommit themselves to developing more appropriate norms will be made. Evaluating norms raises issues of profound importance as to what is responsible and meaningful treatment by the therapist for the involuntarily hospitalized psychiatric patient and his or her family.

REFERENCES

Allen, R. F., & Kraft, C. (1980). *Beat the system: A way to create more human environments.* New York: McGraw Hill.

Allen, R. F., & Kraft, C. (1982). *The organizational unconscious: How to create the corporate culture you want and need.* Englewood Cliffs, NJ: Prentice-Hall.

Falloon, I. R. H., Boyd, L. J., McGill, C. W., Razani, J., Moss, H. B., & Guilderman, A. M. (1982). Family management in the prevention of exacerbation of schizophrenia. *New England Journal of Medicine, 306*(24), 1437-1440.

Goldstein, M. I. (1981). Editor's notes. *New Direction in Mental Health Services: New Developments in Interventions with Families of Schizophrenics, 12,* 1-4.

Halleck, S. M. (1982). Covert values in the treatment of psychosis. *American Journal of Psychotherapy, 35*(2).

Hatfield, A. B. (1979). The family as partner in the treatment of mental illness. *Hospital and Communtiy Psychiatry, 30*(5), 338-340.

Minkoff, K. (1979). A map of chronic mental patients. In J. Talbott (Ed.), *The chronic mental patient* (pp. 11-37). Washington, DC: American Psychiatric Association.

Stein, L. I., & Test, M. A. (1982). Community treatment of the young adult patient. *New Directions for Mental Health Services: The Young Adult Chronic Patient, 14,* 57-67.

Comment

At Fair Oaks Hospital we have found that commitment to treatment is not necessary in order to effectively care for involuntarily hospitalized patients.

Most involuntary patients are hospitalized because of behavior which is out of control (Hall et al., 1981). After they are admitted, the first step in treating these patients is behavioral management. This is achieved by placing the patient on a locked unit and judicious use of medications. As soon as behavioral control is accomplished, patient and staff become less frightening to each other and they are better able to talk. From this point on, we make sure that patients understand that involuntary hospitalization is not a punishment, but that it is a strong message from their families and society that their illness is so severe that it must be treated.

Out-of-control behavior does not necessarily mean that a patient has a mental illness. Hall et al. have shown that 43% of involuntary psychiatric admissions to a State Hospital in Texas had medical illnesses which either caused or exacerbated their psychiatric symptoms. The illnesses can range from unusual epilepsies to diabetes to infections to poisoning with heavy metals (Estroff & Gold, 1984; Jefferson & Marshall, 1981).

For these reasons, the next step is an intensive search for treatable causative medical illness. Only if the investigation proves negative is a psychiatric diagnosis made.

This diagnosis is confirmed using modern neuroendocrine tests such as diurnal cortisol, dexamethosone suppression tests and the TRH: TSH stimulation test to demonstrate the biological components of the patient's psychiatric disorder. When the results of these thorough medical and psychiatric evaluations are presented to involuntary patients, they are often more likely to acknowledge their psychiatric illness and to become more compliant with treatment. In addition many involuntary patients are not treatable with psychoanalytic or insight-oriented therapies. Instead they respond much better to supportive and behaviorally based treatment. This is especially true if the patient's family is involved in the treatment process, as is pointed out in Dr. Parson's paper.

If all of these measures fail and the involuntary patient still refuses to cooperate with therapy and/or medications, long-acting injectable antipsychotic medication such as prolixin (Fluphenazine) decanoate can be given once or twice a month and may reduce psychosis sufficiently to allow the patient to be more cooperative with the above-mentioned therapies. If these points are well understood by the treating hospital staff, they tend less to view involuntary patients as "hostile," "unmanageable," or "hopeless." When these practical evaluation and treatment approaches are used at Fair Oaks Hospital we find increased compliance with treatment and less repeat hospitalizations occurring.

Todd Wilk Estroff, M.D.

REFERENCES

Estroff, T. W., & Gold, M. S. (1984). Psychiatric misdiagnosis. In M. S. Gold, R. B. Lydiard, & J. S. Carman (Eds.), *Advances in psychopharmacology: Predicting and improving treatment responses.* Florida: CRC Press.

Hall, R. C. W., Gardner, E. R., Popkin, M. K., et al. (1981). Unrecognized physical illness prompting psychiatric admission: A prospective study. *American Journal of Psychiatry, 138,* 629.

Jefferson, J. W., & Marshall, J. R. (1981). *Neuropsychiatric features of medical disorders.* New York: Plenum Press.

The Uncommitted Patient and the Life-Cycle Crises: An Eriksonian Perspective

Steven R. Heyman

"The Uncommitted Patient," the theme of this journal issue, presents a complex challenge to the therapist. It is often frustrating for a therapist to experience a client who never truly engages in the therapeutic process; who is sporadic in attendance; who "shops around," changing therapists repeatedly; or who seems devoted to therapy but who achieves little. Understanding this client is important, for without understanding, the therapist may never be able to facilitate the client's ultimate engagement in therapy. It is also possible for a therapist to personalize the patient's behavior, so that interpretations of resistance or transference may miss the key dynamics of the client. Although for some clients the uncommitted pattern may be conscious and deliberate, for others it may be a part of a broader situational crisis or life-style, not really in the client's awareness. It may also be that the same issues bringing people to therapy contribute to the uncommitted pattern. Therapist's interpretations, perhaps because of the personalized or countertransference reactions, may amount to "blaming the victim" (Rappaport, 1975; Ryan, 1971). The purpose of this essay is to develop examples of patterns that may contribute to the expression of uncommittedness in patients. Such possibilities, it is hoped, will contribute not only to an understanding of the uncommitted patient, but to ways in which therapy might proceed.

The viewpoint of this essay is based on the epigenetic view of psychosocial development pioneered by Erik Erikson. Trained as an analyst, Erikson (1964) does not dispute the importance of the pregenital stages in the development of personality and psychopathology. He is an ego analyst, however, and assumes a stronger position for the ego than did Freud. Instead of the five conventional stages developed by Freud, Erikson (1959) conceptualizes eight stages of development, which have psychosocial demands with specific life crises connected with them. Out-

Steven R. Heyman, Ph.D., graduated from Louisiana State University. He is presently an assistant professor at the University of Wyoming in Laramie.

comes of these stages may be, in varying degrees, positive or negative, which will influence one's relationship to oneself and to psychosocial realities. These eight stages are summarized in Table 1. Although he conceptualizes eight different stages, they are not discontinuous, unrelated events. The resolution of any given crisis is not fixed at the completion of a stage, but the patterns of resolution will also be affected by later personal and psychosocial factors. Each stage does have its own dynamics, but each will be conditioned and shaped by past crises and resolutions (Smelser, 1980). For Erikson, therapy involves not only a facilitating of resolutions for past conflicts, but also helping utilize the new strengths of each developmental phase that accompany the added vulnerabilities. "Each stage adds something specific to all later ones and makes a new ensemble out of all earlier ones" (Erikson, cited in Evans, 1981, p. 41). Although an analyst, Erikson cautions, "if everything 'goes back' into childhood then everything is somebody else's fault and trust in one's power of taking responsibility for oneself may be undermined" (p. 31). Erikson also responds to those who might move too far from the consequences of de-

Table 1

Summary of Erikson's Developmental Stages

Stage	Related Psycho-analytic stage	Psychosocial Crisis	Outcome Strengths
Oral-sensory	Oral	Basic trust vs. Mistrust	Hope
Anal-muscular	Anal	Autonomy vs. Shame and Doubt	Will
Phallic-locomotor	Phallic	Initiative vs. Guilt	Purpose
Latency	Latency	Industry vs. Guilt	Competence
Adolescence		Identity vs. Confusion	Fidelity
Young Adulthood	Genital	Intimacy vs. Isolation	Love
Middle Adulthood		Generativity vs. Stagnation	Care
Old Age		Integrity vs. Despair	Wisdom

velopmental crises. In discussing the "pop" existentialism of the 1960s, Erikson (1968) assumes "the danger of all existentialism which chooses to remain juvenile is that it shirks the responsibility for the generational process, and thus advocates an abortive human identity" (p. 41). In relation to this, and to a lack of commitment not only in therapy but also in life, Erikson (1964) also states "to live as a philosophical 'stranger' in Camus's sense is one of the choices of mature man; to have that choice the immature person must, with our help, first find a home in the actuality of work and love" (p. 99).

For Erikson, personality and behavior must be understood in the light of both the consequences of the past and the psychosocial demands of the present. Such understanding may be critical with the uncommitted patient. Erikson (1964) states "there are certain stages in the life cycle when even seemingly malignant disturbances are more profitably treated as aggravated life crises rather than as diseases subject to routine psychiatric diagnosis" (p. 65). He underscores this with discussions of how ego-identity problems in war veterans, and with adolescents, have been diagnosed mistakenly as psychopathy (Erikson, 1968). Addressing both past and present crises for patients, Erikson (1968) sees change as occurring when the patient "is put in a position to accept the historical necessity which made him what he is" (p. 74).

Within this framework, the uncommitted behaviors of a client will be discussed in terms of life-cycle factors which may contribute to the disposition to behave in these ways. It is expected that even where the behaviors may seem to be the same across ages, each developmental crisis gives them a particular meaning for the client.

EARLY DEVELOPMENT

It will not be possible to discuss the contributions of each of the first four stages to all of the other stages, but some of the key elements of these initial stages, particularly as they can be related to uncommittedness in therapy will be highlighted here. Rather than being seen only as causes of later behavior, it would be more consistent with Erikson's writings to see them as shaping later patterns, but their specific expression would also be shaped by the psychosocial crisis in the client's present history.

Oral-sensory. For a patient to become involved with, and committed to therapy, minimal levels of basic trust are required. Many individuals lacking in these levels will not engage in therapy. Others may come, but stay only briefly. If the therapist does not have a grasp of the fundamental fearful misanthropy of such clients it is easy for the therapist to act in ways which confirm the patient's mistrust. In other instances the patient's inability to relax and show mutual trust is revealed in attempts to control therapy by duress rather than to have a reciprocal relationship (Erikson, 1959). It may appear as though the client is not committed to therapy, and is intent only on battling the therapist, when it may be that these are the only mechanisms by which the patient may feel trust in a situation. A barometer for such cases is the hope a client has for the encounter. If hope is "the enduring belief of the attainability of fervent wishes" (Erikson, 1964, p. 118), then in its absence we may see the primitive urges and rages which mark the beginning of existence. For the patient who has not been able to develop reasonable trust also has no real hope. Throughout life, for such individuals, attempts at trust have failed and hope has been frustrated. It is the therapeutic task with such clients to develop gradually, in opposition to their history, a setting in which trust and hope can develop. Until this occurs one may see the uncommitted behaviors motivated by fear, rage, and disappointment, but may not understand their source.

Anal-muscular. From this stage several patterns may contribute to uncommitted behaviors. Shame and doubt may prevent the client from coming to therapy, or from being completely candid in therapy. The individual questions personal ability "to face" others, and "hides" even in the therapeutic situation. When such clients consider terminating abruptly, it is often because, having not been candid, or having lied, they feel unable to confront themselves or the therapist.

In other cases the client maintains an "in and out" relationship to therapy. Perhaps more common in college counseling settings or mental health centers than in private practice, the client comes sporadically. When they seem to begin to become involved they miss sessions. The quality of actions in such cases reflects an inability to maintain a sense of autonomy and self-control. If the client gives up the attempts of autonomy and truly engages in therapy, feelings of powerlessness and concealed shame and doubt will emerge (Erikson, 1963). If successful resolution of this stage leads to will, "willfullness," in a childlike sense, is a reflection of a poor resolution. The struggle between forced choice and forced restraint shows itself in the "in and out" pattern.

Lastly, shame and doubt can lead to a compulsive life-style, and these patterns find their way to therapy. The client produces much, yet little seems to get done. While a similar pattern in content may reflect a later stage (industry vs. inferiority), the quality from this earlier stage is more of a production that attempts to hide or undo feelings of shame and doubt, as opposed to "I am what I produce," more typical of the later stage.

Phallic-locomotor. The positive outgrowth of this stage is initiative and purpose, "the courage to envisage and pursue valued goals uninhibited by the defeat of infantile fantasies, by guilt, and by the foiling fear of punishment" (Erikson, 1964, p. 122). For those who do not have as successful a completion of this stage, therapy may force them to confront their guilt, and in so doing may be so threatening that as this occurs their commitment to therapy waivers. Other clients manifest "false starts," where they come and work, initially with energy and vigor, only to withdraw.

In the positive outcome of this stage initiative will add to autonomy a focusing quality, the ability to undertake, plan, and attack a task. With a less positive outcome, the client in therapy, rather than leaving or becoming sporadic, may seem to challenge the therapist continually. Unlike the pattern of basic mistrust, it does not have the primitive sense of emotion and rage, but is a more reasoned attack. With more clearly developed phallic qualities clients may come to therapy with idealism and enthusiasm disproportionate to the slow pace with which therapy proceeds. The reasoned attack may follow this, both in response to disappointment and to the surfacing of feelings of guilt which the enthusiasm may have kept hidden.

Latency. Until this point there is not as much to divide Erikson from more classical analysts. Beginning with this stage, Erikson assumes that important forces continue to shape the individual, rather than such events being epiphenomena, reflective only of past stages.

Latency is the longest of the preadolescent stages. In the development of industry versus inferiority, the client comes to learn of personal value in the world. Tasks are given in play, at school, and with peers. For some children it is a chance to discover worth beyond what parents have provided, while for others, without the family's protection, there is the discovery of how comparatively less valued they are by others. There may also be a continued sense of defeat for individuals with poor outcomes of other stages. The sense of inferiority developed during this period may lead a client to avoid therapy, which would, in the admission of problems others do not have, add to the sense of inferiority. Where an artificial sense of competence has been developed by work, by production, there is a sense of obligation without enjoyment. Such mechanical productivity may surface in therapy, with little true gain or change, and in a clear way, with little commitment to the process of therapy. If the sense of inferiority is too exposed, or becomes too rapidly exposed, the ability of the individual to remain committed to therapy can be thrown in jeopardy.

THE LATER LIFE CRISES AND UNCOMMITTED PATIENTS

Adolescence. Thus far suggestions as to the roots of uncommitted patterns have been sketched from Erikson's discussions of the earlier life stages. Again, these stages are not discontinuous, but flow into each other. Most clients will express not so much one "pure root," but interactions between previous stages and current psychosocial demands. To view only the past would be too extensive a reduction, perhaps finding one tree in a forest.

Of the life stages in which uncommitted behaviors are perhaps most often shown, and which may have the greatest number of contributory causes, is adolescence. Much from childhood may be reactivated, yet the adult personality has not yet formed consolidated patterns (Blos, 1972; 1980).

Adolescence, for Erikson, is the stage during which the development of a basic sense of identity should occur, although the possibility remains for this not to occur, and a pervading sense of confusion or alternatively negative outcomes may result. As was stated previously, Erikson (1963) observes that the negative outcomes at this and at other stages may lead to behaviors mistakenly seen as more pathological. It is often hard for the therapist working with adolescents to differentiate more severe identity confusion from borderline conditions. It is not in the scope of this paper to address this issue, but it is an important one.

The domains that are the most confusing to the adolescent—personal identity and meaning, sexual identity, vocational choice, and so many others—are also the likely topics in therapy. While in a long-term sense their examination can lead to resolution of conflicts and growth, the act of expression of these confusions, and attempts at confrontation of them, may lead to added fear and turmoil, so that the adolescent drops out of therapy, or shows other uncommitted behaviors. Erikson (1968) discusses the political arena as one in which adolescents may search for identity. There are adolescents who do the same in therapy, "shopping around" for a magical solution. Some may develop cult-like identifications with forms of therapy or therapists, while others may join cults, in both cases with little real commitment to self-examination. Fortunately, for most adolescents the inauthenticity of these attempts will eventually cause them to continue their search; regrettably, a minority are worsened by these experiences.

Blos (1972) eloquently makes the case that the adolescent's relationship to therapy is misunderstood. What are defined as uncommitted behaviors in this essay, according to Blos, may be seen by therapists as a negative therapeutic reaction or massive resistance, when, in fact, they are part of the "holding pattern" of adolescence. Adolescents may abruptly decide to leave therapy, even when work has been proceeding well (Blos, 1980), as part of the discontinuous nature of identity development. Blos indicates how he deals with these behaviors, which includes an acceptance of them. Following is an illustrative case of mine.

> Carl, a 19-year-old construction worker, came to therapy "to find" himself. In the first few sessions he spoke of himself and his family. A bright young man, no one in his family had shown intellectual or aesthetic sensitivity. As the third of five brothers from a poor farming family he had learned to be tough, aggressive, and achievement

oriented. His growing sense of "missing" and "being empty" was intense. After six sessions, in which we explored his conflicts with family, peers, and values, he did not return, later calling to say he was "thinking things over." He was encouraged to do so, and the possibility of returning to therapy was emphasized. Two months later he did return. For five sessions he worked at sorting out his feelings, and then asked "to take some time off." About 4 weeks later he returned. This pattern continued over 7 months, after which he was seen in therapy continuously for 4 months. His personal growth during this period was amazing. He started college the following fall, and was able to develop a very deep, meaningful relationship with a girlfriend. During therapy, especially in the last segment, he mentioned how important it had been for him to take time off, and then be able to return.

In Carl's case, the uncommitted behaviors corresponded to periods of examination and consolidation, setting the stage for another period of work. Rather than seeing him as an uncommitted patient, these behaviors are seen as a reflection of the psychosocial crisis of adolescence. The sporadic attendance in therapy was a reflection of the discontinuous nature of identity development.

Another component of the identity confusion is a time confusion (Erikson, 1968). The present has an expansive, involving quality, and the progress of past sessions or the demarcation of a future appointment are less real. The client may miss several appointments, and then seek one urgently, as though unaware the therapist has other commitments. Again, what may be judged as "uncommitted" behaviors may be a reflection of this time orientation. Similarly, in order to become committed to therapy there must be a conviction that there is time enough for change. This trust in time, as part of time confusion, may be absent. Also, the client may display alternating feelings of being very old, filled with despair, or very young and childlike, too immature to work.

In addition to identity confusion, another outcome of the adolescent crisis presents clear therapeutic challenges. The "negative identity" involves "identifications and roles which, at critical stages of development have been presented to the individual as most undesirable and dangerous, and yet also as the most real" (Erikson, 1959, p. 29). Here we find the delinquent, the "street people," and many others. We are again confronted with sorting out stage-related identity issues from more pathological patterns.

Negative-identity individuals almost always at first seem totally uncommitted to therapy, particularly if coerced into it. An "all pervasive mockery which characterizes the initial therapeutic contact with these patients who . . . trust nothing but mistrust" (Erikson, 1959, p. 134). Such

patients may show their seeming uncommittedness in irregular attendance, in searching for a therapist more in agreement with their values, or
in a resistant stance in therapy. Therapists who have worked with such
clients come to recognize that beyond these behaviors reflective of current confusions and past misfortunes, they "watch from a dark corner of
the mind (and indeed often from the corner of an eye) for new experiences simple and forthright enough to permit a renewal of the most
basic experiments in trustful mutuality" (Erikson, 1959, p. 134).

The client who has a negative identity presents a particular bind for the
therapist. The negative identity is likely self-defeating, and yet to give it
up is even more of a crisis, for, in a real sense, it is all the identity they
have. Some therapists quickly try to accentuate what they see as positive
identity components. Such statements, suggestions, or foci are very
threatening to the identity network of such adolescents, opposite in effect
to the intended therapeutic intent. Protection from failure and frustration
has occurred because of this negative system. Not only are the positive in-
puts simply dissonant with their sense of identity, they may relate to, or
activate, threatening images. Such clients will lessen their commitment to
therapy in the face of such threat.

For these complex problems Erikson points towards possible approaches. The therapist must accept the client's identity as *real and necessary,* "without concluding . . . it is 'all there is' " (Erikson, 1968, p.
215). Through periods of testing, what will most probably include the
seemingly uncommitted patterns, the therapist must be able to maintain an
understanding and regard for the client, without engulfing the client or
being engulfed.

> In rural western Oklahoma a mother brought her 16-year-old son to
> therapy. He was "constantly" getting into fistfights, and with
> friends was engaging in petty thefts. He was average in appearance,
> dressed in a black denim jacket, and wearing a black felt cowboy hat
> (very common in Oklahoma), with the overall appearance of being
> under a dark cloud. At first sullen and withdrawn, little real com-
> munication came from him. It was possible to engage in conversa-
> tions, but not in therapy. At the time, the movie *Urban Cowboy* had
> been released, and he began to discuss it. By the end of our second
> session discussing the movie it was clear to both of us whom we
> were discussing. He missed 2 weeks, and when he came back he
> was angry, expressing a sense of frustration, rage, and hinting at
> termination. I accepted his feelings, but indicated any decisions
> about termination would be his. Whom he saw in *Urban Cowboy,* in
> our discussions, was too threatening. He did not return for several
> weeks, and then called to ask about rescheduling. He was told he
> could, but did not set up an appointment with the secretary. After

several more weeks he returned and talked about some minor trouble in which he and some friends had been involved. Although many directions were possible, we began discussing the word "adventure" that he used at the beginning of that session. For the next few sessions he was reluctant to pursue the issues in depth, but gradually began to do so.

The "uncommitted" behaviors this client showed again seemed consistent with the identity issues with which he was grappling. After another year in therapy, he graduated from high school, and took a job as a ranchhand, keeping in a job with diversity and adventure. He also became a Big Brother and in this relationship worked on, and made up for, previously unresolved issues.

Adolescents, coming to therapy, regardless of the veneers of strength or hostility which they may erect, often know these structures are a Potemkin village. Faced with a successful adult therapist, who they expect knows more about them than they would like to reveal, they are particularly inclined to use uncommitted behaviors as an "identity resistance" (Erikson, 1959, p. 135), fearing the therapist may carelessly or deliberately destroy their fragile sense of identity, perhaps by imposing an identity. Kahn (1968) agrees with Erikson, and adds that the fluidity of their defenses and unstable identities are troublesome for therapists seeking more routine and commitment in the behaviors of clients. Kahn also agrees with Erikson as to the need for affection and understanding with these clients; a subtlety or restrained quality may be critical so that therapy does not become too close initially or too threatening.

It must be noted that the uncommitted pattern, particularly for the adolescent, may have uniquely important secondary gains. In the adolescent moratorium the commitment to limited possibilities may seem less valuable than the unlimited possibilities in chaos. Despite the isolation there is a sense of uniqueness, with suffering conveying a special sensitivity. No matter how artificial these behaviors or beliefs may seem, this may be the total conscious identity of the client. Although the trappings of philosophy, literature, or politics present fewer immediate problems than delinquency, they may cloak an essentially negative identity. The uncommitted behaviors may convey a recognition of what is to be lost if engagement with therapy occurs.

Therapy with adolescents is made additionally difficult in that the qualities required for true commitment may have not yet developed, and the problems in their development may be reflected in the uncommitted behaviors. Fidelity, a positive outcome of adolescence, "is the ability to sustain loyalties freely pledged in spite of the inevitable contradictions of value systems" (Erikson, 1964, p. 125). Fidelity is an important precondition for commitment to therapy, and though lacking in the individual it may be required for therapy. The compromise, or perhaps the necessity, is the uncommitted behavior.

The ability to truly engage with another is the result and test of a firm identity delineation (Erikson, 1959), and where it is missing relationships may take on a desperate quality. When the relationship appears to fail there may be an intense wish to start over again, perhaps with another therapist.

If the seemingly uncommitted behaviors can be understood, when appropriate, for the instances in which they reflect components of this psychosocial crisis, it becomes easier to develop an understanding, sincere partnership with adolescents, even if it means allowing them to terminate or interrupt therapy (Blos, 1972). If "truly worthwhile acts enhance a mutuality between the doer and the other—a mutuality which strengthens the doer even as it strengthens the other" (Erikson, 1964, p. 233), the understanding of these stage-related behaviors may well facilitate a growth and development, with the adolescent working on therapeutic issues while working on identity issues. As Blos (1972) reports, these seemingly uncommitted patients return to therapy after abrupt terminations when they are better able to work on the issues with which they have struggled privately. The therapist's previous actions will likely determine the client's willingness to return. If misperceived, and dealt with inappropriately, the uncommitted client may seek elsewhere. As Erikson (1959) notes, the confused adolescent does maintain "a readiness to repudiate, to isolate, and if necessary to destroy those forces and people whose essence seems dangerous" (p. 195) to them.

Young Adulthood. Although with young adults some of the raging storms of adolescence must continue, for most a basic resolution to the identity conflicts will have occurred, and there will be a consolidation of patterns. In therapy, as in life, the issues of intimacy become critical. "The danger of this stage is that intimate, competitive, and combatative relations are experienced with and against the same people" (Erikson, 1963, p. 264). The uncommitted behaviors at this stage reflect the intimacy problems. They may show both in exclusivity, a desire for a special relationship with the client (sexual, emotional, or personal), and in rejectivity, active or passive hostility and withdrawal from therapy when angered or frustrated (Erikson, 1982). Individuals at this stage are prone to search for "isolation à deux" (Erikson, 1963, p. 266), a relationship with what can be called "pseudointimacy." Even where therapy has been progressing, if the intimacy issues are strong, and the client meets someone who seems suddenly magically to fulfill all needs, abrupt termination is possible.

Whereas in adolescence the intimacy issues are only part of a greater confusion, for the young adult they become the central focus. It is easy, perhaps too easy, for the therapist to see transference issues relating to childhood, overlooking the importance of these issues at this particular stage. Another danger for the therapist is that the intimacy crisis and the uncommitted behaviors may be seen as reflective of a schizoid process, as opposed to the developmental crisis. This cannot be resolved with an "either-or" judgment, but requires considerable attention to history and past crisis resolution, as well as to the psychosocial stage demands.

Middle Adulthood. Clients in middle adulthood are often highly dedicated, due at least in part to their recognition of the need for change before it "is too late." For others, however, therapy may again ask the client to engage in behaviors which are difficult for them. Stagnation, the negative outcome of this stage, is likely to involve a personal impoverishment, a self-indulgence, and the use of physical symptoms as a means of expressing self-concern (Erikson, 1959). Trapped in a quicksand pit of their own design, evasion and uncommittedness may be the solutions. "Regression from generativity to an obsessive need for pseudo-intimacy takes place, often with a pervading sense of impoverishment" (Erikson, 1959, p. 97). When hoped-for solutions do not come, whimsical, self-indulgent, childlike patterns may be seen (Erikson, 1959), including missed appointments.

King (1980) notes that in midlife adolescent crises may be relived or reexperienced, whether or not early or infantile material is dealt with. "At both phases of the life cycle, adolescence and midlife, he has to adjust to sexual and biological changes . . . conflicts about dependence and independence, which are also experienced during adolescence" (King, 1980, p. 156) become themes in the work of, and uncommittedness of, midlife clients.

Although the midlife adult in crisis may show some of the same qualities of the adolescent, the psychosocial implications are far more serious. Typically, there has been a considerable involvement with career and family, as opposed to the beginning of all these in adolescence. Although there may be new beginnings for the person in midlife, they will be more costly because of ruptures with past decades. Propelled, perhaps, by a sense of urgency, there may be an ambivalence in the considerations of loss in change, with uncommitted patterns an expression of this conflict.

> Cora, a 46-year-old teacher, had been married for 25 years, a condition she described as "passable." Little seemed worthwhile to her. In therapy she provided many rationalizations, but few indications of a willingness to take responsibility. At first regular in therapy, she became irregular, returning twice after having seen other therapists. In her third foray she found an unlicensed, untrained individual who practiced "psychotherapy" through a legal loophole. She completely submerged herself not only in "therapy," but in the "foundation" he ran. Unlike the adolescent who might try this and

then move on, Cora stayed with it, having found something external to relieve her feelings of stagnation. The possible gains from therapy were outweighed for her by risks.

Late Adulthood. Until very recently little attention in the therapy literature has dealt with the problems of these clients, and the problems of therapists with these clients (King, 1980; 1982). The dominant feature of the uncommitted patient at this stage is despair. The uncommittedness and despair take two major forms. The client may come to therapy, but refuses to engage, often seeming to do no more than vent despair. Whether they continue in this pattern or terminate, the shroud of despair seems to be between them and commitment to therapy.

Such clients are difficult for therapists at personal levels for several reasons. Their despair may be contagious. They may accuse the therapist of being too young to understand. It is easy for such clients to arouse countertransferences relating to the therapist's parents. Major life changes in these patients are unlikely, and they do not have the characteristics of the ideal patient ("YAVIS") described by Schofield (1964). Therapists may be relieved by their uncommittedness, particularly if its place in the life cycle is not seen.

> Elaine, a 71-year-old woman, was brought to therapy by her granddaughter. She had been seen several times the previous year by a therapist who described her as "obstinate, depressed, and presenile." Her husband had died 2 years before, and she was gradually withdrawing from activities. In the first four sessions, held over 2½ months, she did little more than weep, complain, and sit silently. She missed various appointments, making sure I knew her return was only for her granddaughter. In one session we discussed her sense of loss of her own beauty and adolescence. She sparkled as she described her enjoyment of acting, and noted there were auditions upcoming for the community theater. For that session and the next we discussed acting, expression, and life. She gained courage, and auditioned for a small part in the play, in which she was cast. She continued in therapy, sporadically during rehearsals, working slowly on issues in her life. After the play ended she was regular in therapy for 6 months, and her despair diminished, replaced by a gusto. She became a crisis phone volunteer, and also worked at a senior citizens center, with "the old folks." She was able to address longstanding conflicts with her daughter, who was so inspired she sought therapy and was referred to a colleague.

Despair leading to uncommitted behaviors may be seen throughout the life cycle. In late adulthood, however, the despair has a psychosocial validity unmatched at other ages. While understanding the despair and its manifestations in the lack of commitment in an older individual may not insure the success of therapy, it is perhaps the best possible option.

SUMMARY

It has been difficult to keep this paper within the boundaries of the topic and length requirements. Of necessity, the summary must be brief.

Erikson, as a psychoanalyst, accepts the fundamental importance of the early stages of childhood to later personality and psychopathology, but he also sees these as having more features than did classical psychoanalytic thought. Rather than personality being largely set by the end of the phallic stage, Erikson posits five additional stages, each with its psychosocial demands, developmental crises, and possible positive and negative outcomes. Each stage has implications for continued personality development. The stages are not discontinuous, however, and blend and flow with each other. Resolutions to conflicts at any stage are not necessarily permanent, and are influenced by the continued vicissitudes of the individual's developmental crises.

Within this perspective, although uncommitted behaviors may seem the same across the life cycle, the meaning and motivations for such behaviors may vary greatly. To evaluate these behaviors against only the earliest stages of development, or only in relationship to the therapist, may underestimate not only the uncommitted behaviors but the developmental crisis of the client as well. Such an underestimation will impair the likelihood of an eventually successful therapeutic outcome.

The very components of the developmental life crises that propel clients into therapy present a serious paradox. The developmental crisis may revolve around the very behaviors that are required for a commitment to therapy. It may be easier at times for the therapist to blame the client for the uncommitted behaviors than to understand them, particularly as the uncommitted patient presents a frustrating, and perhaps threatening situation to the therapist. If, however, the uncommitted pattern is reflective of the life crisis, then understanding this may be facilitative not only of an understanding of the client and for a reduction of countertransferences, but also of optimizing the chances for an eventually successful therapy which will deal with the life-crisis issues as they deal with the issues of the uncommitted pattern.

REFERENCES

Adler, G. (1980). Transference, real relationship, and alliance. *International Journal of Psychoanalysis, 61*, 547-558.
Blos, P. (1972). The epigenesis of the adult neurosis. *The Psychoanalytic Study of the Child, 27*, 106-135.

Blos, P. (1980). The life cycle as indicated by the nature of the transference in the psychoanalysis of adolescents. *International Journal of Psychoanalysis, 61,* 145-150.

Erikson, E. H. (1959). Identity and the life cycle. *Psychological Issues, 1,* 1-171.

Erikson, E. H. (1963). *Childhood and society* (2nd ed.). New York: W. W. Norton.

Erikson, E. H. (1964). *Insight and responsibility.* New York: W. W. Norton.

Erikson, E. H. (1968). *Identity: Youth and crisis.* New York: W. W. Norton.

Erikson, E. H. (1982). *The life cycle completed.* New York: W. W. Norton.

Evans, R. I. (1981). *Dialogue with Erik Erikson.* New York: Praeger.

Kahn, M. D. (1968). The adolescent struggle with identity as a force in psychotherapy. *Adolescence, 3,* 395-424.

King, P. H. M. (1974). Notes on the psychoanalysis of older patients. *Journal of Analytical Psychology, 19,* 22-37.

King, P. (1980). The life cycle as indicated by the nature of the transference in the psychoanalysis of the middle-aged and elderly. *International Journal of Psychoanalysis, 61,* 153-159.

Neugarten, B. L. (1969). Continuities and discontinuities of psychological issues into adult life. *Human Development, 12,* 121-130.

Rappaport, J. (1975). Alternatives to blaming the victim or the environment. *American Psychologist, 30,* 525-528.

Ryan, W. (1971). *Blaming the victim.* New York: Random House.

Schofield, W. (1964). *Psychotherapy: The purchase of friendship.* Englewood Cliffs, NJ: Prentice Hall.

Smelser, N. J. (1980). Issues in the study of work and love in adulthood. In N. J. Smelser & E. H. Erikson (Eds.), *Themes of work and love in adulthood.* Cambridge, MA: Harvard University Press.

Stiles, W. B. (1979). Psychotherapy recapitulates ontogeny: The epigenesis of intensive interpersonal relationships. *Psychotherapy: Theory, research, practice, 16,* 391-403.

Comment

This article nicely elaborates the many potential meanings associated with uncommitted patient behavior. The eight Eriksonian life stages provide theory to generate many possibilities for how life-crisis issues are enacted as resistance to treatment. As such, uncommitted behavior becomes salient in and of itself, and commands understanding and treatment for its own sake. I think this represents a core awareness for any practicing psychotherapist: that what interferes with interactive process may require respect, not the combative assault of a "conquer and get rid of" attitude.

In order to make this point I think a straw dog is created by implying that the traditional psychodynamic perspective regards resistance as an intentional thwarting by the patient, which needs to be overcome and destroyed by the therapist, so that treatment can proceed, whereas many early psychoanalytic thinkers came to view resistance as being present for good reason. Reich, for one example, wrote in the 1920s about character resistance as the main meal of treatment.

From a broader outlook, then, resistance represents eventual blocks against healthy, natural responsiveness to life. In my experience, whether uncommitted patient behavior is resistance always remains an obscure speculation until afterwards. The decision to continue in treatment, for example, in its fullest glory represents an existential leap into the unknown. It can symbolize either affirmation of life or a denigration of the human spirit. I posture this decision so that it falls in the client's lap. I try to present the most completely balanced arguments available for how termination may be evasion or how it may be essential to growth, and then wait.

I agree wholeheartedly with the author that noncommitted behavior per se is not an evil recalcitrant resistance to be eradicated. I would go further than that and say it is worth our reflection as psychotherapists to note many more healthy reasons why nonengagement with our professional activity can denote a sane decision in favor of existence, not resistance. Decreased spendable time and income, and the excuse of being in treatment can obviously diminish one's engagement in real-life decisions. Besides the pathology of escapism, the client may become freed of maintaining a delusion that the relationship is helpful. In fact, the liberated client may find that he or she no longer needs to jump through unproductive hoops constructed by a misunderstanding therapist, and is not saddled by the problems of the therapist as well as one's own.

Darrell Dawson, Ph.D.